Frank Moosmann

AF239022

**Interlacing Self-Localization, Moving Object Tracking
and Mapping for 3D Range Sensors**

Schriftenreihe
Institut für Mess- und Regelungstechnik,
Karlsruher Institut für Technologie (KIT)

Band 024

Eine Übersicht über alle bisher in dieser Schriftenreihe erschienenen Bände finden Sie am Ende des Buchs.

Interlacing Self-Localization, Moving Object Tracking and Mapping for 3D Range Sensors

by
Frank Moosmann

 Scientific Publishing

Dissertation, Karlsruher Institut für Technologie
Fakultät für Maschinenbau
Tag der mündlichen Prüfung: 26. Oktober 2012
Referenten: Prof. Dr.-Ing. C. Stiller, Prof. Dr.-Ing. K. Dietmayer

Impressum

Karlsruher Institut für Technologie (KIT)
KIT Scientific Publishing
Straße am Forum 2
D-76131 Karlsruhe
www.ksp.kit.edu

KIT – Universität des Landes Baden-Württemberg und nationales
Forschungszentrum in der Helmholtz-Gemeinschaft

KIT Scientific Publishing 2013
Print on Demand

ISSN 1613-4214
ISBN 978-3-86644-977-0

Interlacing Self-Localization, Moving Object Tracking and Mapping for 3D Range Sensors

Zur Erlangung des akademischen Grades eines

Doktors der Ingenieurwissenschaften

von der Fakultät für Maschinenbau
des Karlsruher Instituts für Technologie (KIT)
genehmigte

Dissertation

von

DIPL.-INFORM. FRANK MOOSMANN

aus Karlsruhe

Hauptreferent: Prof. Dr.-Ing. C. Stiller
Korreferent: Prof. Dr.-Ing. K. Dietmayer
Tag der mündlichen Prüfung: 26. Oktober 2012

Vorwort

Meinem Doktorvater Prof. Dr.-Ing. Christoph Stiller danke ich für die Betreuung dieser Arbeit, das in mich gesetzte Vertrauen und die mir gestatteten Freiheiten. Insbesondere das hervorragend organisierte Institut und die Möglichkeiten zum Auslandsaufenthalt, zu Konferenzbesuchen und zur Teilnahme an der Grand Cooperative Driving Challenge habe ich sehr geschätzt. Mein Dank gilt außerdem Herrn Prof. Dr.-Ing. Klaus Dietmayer für die Übernahme des Korreferats und Herrn Prof. Dr.-Ing. Marcus Geimer für die Übernahme des Prüfungsvorsitzes.

Dem Karlsruher House of Young Scientists danke ich für die finanzielle Unterstützung meines sechsmonatigen Forschungsaufenthaltes in Grenoble und Thierry Fraichard für die Einladung in seine Forschungsgruppe. Außerdem danke ich der Deutschen Forschungsgesellschaft, die diese Arbeit im Rahmen des Sonderforschungsbereich/Transregio 28 finanziell unterstützt hat.

Einen wesentlichen Einfluss auf die Arbeit hatten meine Kollegen, Hiwis, Diplom- und Studienarbeiter. Die Zusammenarbeit war sehr lehrreich und hat mir viel Spaß bereitet. Danke! Im Speziellen danke ich Andreas, Andrew, Hannes, Henning, Julius, Martin, Tobias und Xavier, die mir hilfreiches Feedback zur Ausarbeitung bzw. zum Vortrag gegeben haben.

Ganz besonderer Dank gilt meinen Freunden, meiner Familie und vor allem meiner Frau Carola. Die Zeit mit euch konnte ich sehr genießen und gab mir immer neue Kraft und Motivation!

Karlsruhe, im Dezember 2012   Frank Moosmann

Kurzfassung

Autonome Fahrzeuge bieten die Aussicht auf eine erhöhte Verkehrssicherheit, eine erhöhte Effizienz sowie einen erhöhten Fahrkomfort. Diese Verbesserungen werden ermöglicht, da technische Systeme im Gegensatz zu menschlichen Fahrern ermüdungsfrei sind und potentiell eine schnellere Reaktionsfähigkeit bieten. Weitere Möglichkeiten bieten sich durch direkte Kommunikation und Kooperation sowohl zwischen Fahrzeugen als auch zwischen Fahrzeugen und der Infrastruktur.

Eine Hauptkomponente, die für den sicheren Betrieb autonomer Fahrzeuge benötigt wird, ist ein System zur zuverlässigen Umfeldwahrnehmung. Dieses besteht immer aus einer Kombination von Hardware, d.h. Sensoren, und Software. In den letzten Jahren wurden neue Sensoren entwickelt, welche die Umgebung mittels dichter, präziser Entfernungsmessungen dreidimensional abtasten. Bei den dafür verwendeten Algorithmen handelte es sich jedoch oft um angepasste Verfahren von älteren, einfacheren Sensorarten.

Die vorliegende Arbeit beschäftigt sich mit Algorithmen, welche speziell für diese modernen 3D-Sensoren entwickelt wurden. Das hier vorgestellte Gesamtkonzept beinhaltet mehrere Neuheiten: Zunächst werden neuartige Methoden zur Verbesserung der Rohdaten und zum Berechnen von geometrischen Charakteristiken eingeführt. Dies umfasst Verfahren zur Rauschunterdrückung, Verfahren zur Interpolation fehlender Messungen und Verfahren zur Schätzung von Objektkanten, Oberflächenrauheit und -orientierung. Ferner wird eine neuartige Methode zum Erstellen von Objekthypothesen durch Gruppieren von Messungen präsentiert. Jede Gruppierung entspricht dabei einem Bereich der Umgebung, welcher sich eigenständig im Raum bewegen könnte. Das vorgestellte Verfahren greift dabei nicht auf hinterlegte Objektmodelle zurück, sondern ermöglicht das Erkennen jeglicher Verkehrsteilnehmer. Des Weiteren wird ein innovatives Verfahren zur zeitlichen Verfolgung der Objekthypothesen beschrieben. Durch die darin enthaltene Geschwindigkeitsschätzung wird die Vorhersage zukünftiger Positionen aller Verkehrsteilnehmer ermöglicht. Zusätzlich wird die Position und Geschwindigkeit des Eigenfahrzeugs bezüglich der Umgebung berechnet. Dies erlaubt die präzise Bestimmung der Fahrzeugposition selbst in Regionen mit fehlender oder schlechter Satellitenortung (z.B. GPS). Im Verfolgungsschritt integriert ist das dynamische Generieren von 3D Modellen, sowohl von der Umgebung als auch aller bewegten Objekte. Diese könnten zur Erstellung detaillierter dreidimensionaler Karten von Städten oder zum automatisierten Lernen von Objektmodellen weiterverwendet werden.

Die vorgestellten Algorithmen unterscheiden sich von bisherigen Arbeiten durch mehrere Aspekte: Die gemeinsame Behandlung von Lokalisierung und Objektverfolgung ergibt ein robustes Verfahren und ermöglicht eine kompakte Implementierung. Zudem erlaubt der vorgestellte Entwurf, im Gegensatz zu vielen objektspezifischen Ansätzen, das Erkennen beliebiger Verkehrsteilnehmer. Zusätzlich enthält das Verfahren keine Annahmen über die Umgebung und ermöglich daher eine Anwendung in beliebigen Innen- oder Außenräumen.

Zur Verifizierung des vorgestellten Verfahrens dienen Daten eines Laserscanners mit $360°$ Erfassungsbereich, welcher auf dem Dach eines Fahrzeugs in innerstädtischem Umfeld bewegt wurde. Eine qualitative wie auch eine quantitative Analyse zeigen, dass es unter ausschließlicher Verwendung dieser Entfernungsdaten möglich ist das Eigenfahrzeug präzise zu lokalisieren und bewegte Verkehrsteilnehmer zuverlässig zu erkennen und zu verfolgen.

Schlagworte: Objektdetektion – Verfolgung – Selbstlokalisierung – Kartierung – Entfernungsdaten – Laserscanner

Abstract

Autonomous vehicles provide the prospect of increased traffic safety, higher efficiency, and increased driving comfort. These improvements arise from two properties of technical systems: in contrast to human drivers they are fatigue-proof and they potentially have a faster reaction time. Further potential exists by employing communication and cooperation on both the vehicle-to-vehicle and the vehicle-to-infrastructure level.

One key component required for the safe operation of autonomous vehicles is a system for reliably perceiving the environment. Such a perception system is always a combination of hardware, i. e. sensors, and software. In recent years, new sensors were developed that scan the environment by precisely measuring the distance to objects in the vicinity with a high spatial resolution. Current algorithms used for processing data from these sensors typically derive from methods that were designed for older, simpler sensors.

This work focuses on algorithms that are designed for this new class of sensors. Several contributions are made: First, novel methods are introduced for the enhancement of the raw sensor data and for the calculation of geometrical characteristics. This includes methods for noise reduction, methods for interpolating over missing measurements, and methods for estimating object borders, surface roughness, and surface direction. Second, an original method is presented for forming object hypotheses by grouping the distance measurements. Each group thereby corresponds to a region in the environment that could move independently. The presented grouping approach does not use specific object models but enables detecting arbitrary traffic participants. Third, an innovative method is proposed to track these object hypotheses over time. Intrinsically contained is the estimation of their velocity which renders possible the prediction of future positions for all traffic participants. Additionally, the position of the sensor vehicle with respect to the environment is estimated. This facilitates determining the precise position even in regions with low or no GPS coverage. Integrated into tracking is the simultaneous creation of 3D models for both, moving objects and the static environment. These models could be further used for creating detailed 3D city plans or for automatically learning object models.

The proposed algorithms stand out against other works by several aspects: The joint treatment of localization and tracking leads to a robust method and keeps the implementation compact. The generic design enables the detection of arbitrary objects, which stands in contrast to many methods specializing for certain object types. Finally, no assumption is made about the type of environment, which allows for an application within any indoor and outdoor environment.

The successful operation of the proposed methods is verified on data captured with a laser scanner from the top of a moving car in inner-city areas. Qualitative and quantitative analyses show the possibility of precise self-localization and robust moving object detection and tracking using solely distance readings from modern 3D sensors.

Keywords: Object detection – tracking – self-localization – mapping – range data – laser scanner

Contents

Nomenclature

Abbrevations

cf.	compare (*latin: confer*)
e. g.	for example (*latin: exempli gratia*)
et al.	and others (*latin: et alii*)
i. e.	that is (*latin: id est*)
iff	if and only if
radar	radio detection and range
lidar	light detection and range
2D/3D	2/3-dimensional
DOF	degrees of freedom
CS	coordinate system
ICP	iterative closest points
TOF	time of flight
GPS	global positioning system
INS	integrated navigation system
SLAM	simultaneous localization and mapping
MOM	moving object mapping
KF	Kalman filter

Notations

designators	standard, uppercase: A, B, C, ...
functions	standard, lowercase: a, b, c, ...
skalars	italic, lowercase: $a, b, c, \ldots$
vectors	italic, bold, lowercase: $\boldsymbol{a}, \boldsymbol{b}, \boldsymbol{c}, \ldots$
matrices	italic, bold, uppercase: $\boldsymbol{A}, \boldsymbol{B}, \boldsymbol{C}, \ldots$
sets	calligraphic, uppercase: $\mathcal{A}, \mathcal{B}, \mathcal{C}, \ldots$

Symbols

$\mapsto$	maps to
$\rightarrow$	approaches, transition
$\leftarrow$	assignment, transition
$:=$	defines
$\hat{=}$	corresponds to
$\sim$	distributed according to, approximately
$\times$	cross product
$\lvert . \rvert$	cardinality of a set, absolute value, determinant
$\lVert . \rVert$	Euclidean norm
$\{.\}$	set
$\varnothing$	empty set
$\subseteq$	subset
$\cup$	union
$\cap$	intersection
$\wedge$	logical and
$\vee$	logical or
$[.,.]$	closed interval
$(.,.)$	open interval
∂	partial derivative
Δ	change
$\dot{x}$	differential of x with respect to time
$\hat{x}$	estimate of x
$\overline{x}$	average of x
$\boldsymbol{x}^{\mathrm{T}}$	transposed of the vector $\boldsymbol{x}$
$\tilde{x}$	predicted value of x
x', x'', x'''	changed values of x

Variables and Functions

$\arg\{.\}$	argument of a function
$\mathrm{diag}\{.\}$	diagonal of a matrix
$\mathrm{tr}\{.\}$	trace of a matrix, i. e. sum of the diagonal elements
$\mathbf{1}_{\mathcal{A}}(a)$	indicator function = 1 iff $a \in \mathcal{A}$, 0 else

$\mathcal{N}(\mu, \sigma^2)$	normal distribution with mean μ and variance σ^2
$\boldsymbol{I}$	identity matrix
$\boldsymbol{0}$	zero matrix
$\boldsymbol{e}_x, \boldsymbol{e}_y, \boldsymbol{e}_z$	unity vector in x, y, and z respectively
ν	constants
Σ	covariance matrices
$\boldsymbol{\rho}$	6D pose (3 translations, 3 rotations)
ϕ	roll angle (rotation around x axis)
θ	pitch angle (rotation around y axis)
ψ	yaw angle (rotation around z axis)
t	time
w	weight
g, h, i, j, k	indices
u, v	indices in image (column, row)
α, β, γ	angles
r_i	range measurement $\in \mathbb{R}$
$\boldsymbol{p}_i$	point coordinate $\in \mathbb{R}^3$
$\boldsymbol{n}_i$	normal vector $\in \mathbb{R}^3 : \|\boldsymbol{n}_i\| = 1$
f_i	flatness value $\in [0, 1]$
$\boldsymbol{d}_{i,j}$	distance vector $= \boldsymbol{p}_j - \boldsymbol{p}_i$
$l_{i,j}$	linkage value $\in [0, 1]$
$b_{i,j}$	border value $\in [0, 1]$
$c_{i,j}$	convexity value $\in [0, 1]$
$c_{i,j,k}$	triangular convexity $\in [0, 1]$
$c_{i,j}^{\mathrm{x}}$	extended convexity $\in [0, 1]$
$s_{i,j}$	segmentation decision $\in \{true, false\}$
$\mathcal{S}_g$	segment i. e. object hypothesis as set of pixel indices
$\mathcal{P}$	set of 3D points
$\mathcal{N}$	set of normal vectors
$\mathcal{F}$	set of flatness values
$\mathfrak{T}$	track/tracklet
$\mathcal{T}$	set of tracks/tracklets

1 Introduction

Automation has long been at the core of industrialization offering the advantages of increased efficiency, safety, and repeatability (and hence fewer errors). The main focus in automation has always been laid on factory settings since these are well defined and exhibit only few disturbances. Nevertheless, the development reached public life with for example autopilots being in use within aircrafts and ships.

Introducing fully automated driving of cars is just the logical next step. Among the possible benefits are reduced accident rates, increased traffic flow, less pollution, and the possibility to dedicate oneself to other tasks while being in the car. Not surprisingly, research on that topic started decades ago [Dic84, Dic88] and development lead in the meantime to systems like automated distance control [Mar01] or self-parking cars [Kab08]. These systems are already autonomous but still need the driver's attention for their supervision. Although the gap to fully unsupervised automation seems small, serious problems remain. The hardest part is probably a reliable perception of the environment that works during night and daytime and possibly under all weather conditions.

The term *perception* describes a very wide concept, but two main tasks can be identified with respect to autonomous driving: First, a vehicle has to precisely know its current position in order to determine the way it should be going. This task is also known as the *localization* problem. Second, a vehicle has to sense its surroundings and detect static obstacles as well as moving traffic participants. An essential part is thereby the estimation of the velocity of moving objects. This allows the vehicle to predict their future position and to determine which space is free in order to avoid accidents. Only if both components are good enough, safe operation is possible.

The present work is targeted exactly at this challenge. Algorithms for both key ingredients of perception systems are proposed and analyzed: The estimation of the position and orientation of the vehicle and the detection of other traffic participants including the estimation of their motion. By focusing on very recent sensor technology, this work proposes novel ideas and thoroughly evaluates them using the experimental autonomous vehicle AnnieWAY shown in Figure 1.1.

Figure 1.1: The experimental car *AnnieWAY* is equipped with numerous sensors and is capable of driving autonomously. The presented work focuses on data from the top mounted laser scanner and targets at sensing the environment.

Before going into details, the following pages describe the used sensor system and discuss related work. Thereafter, a more detailed overview of the proposed approach is presented.

1.1   Sensor System

Modern cars are already equipped with a variety of sensors to perceive the environment. Active sensors like radar (radio detection and ranging), lidar (light detection and ranging), or ultrasonic sensors directly measure distance – advantageous for safe driving since free space is inherently detected. On the contrary, passive sensors like cameras or infrared cameras are more intuitive to humans and currently excel at providing dense measurements. This allows for a better identification of other traffic participants with the downside of not precisely knowing their distance or velocity. Furthermore, these sensors are heavily affected by environmental conditions. As a consequence, existing systems normally employ several different sensors at the same time in order to compensate for the different disadvantages (see e. g. [Wen08] or [Spi10]).

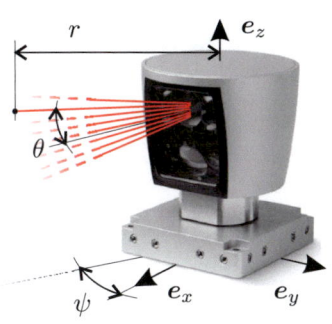 

(a) 3D lidar sensor *Velodyne HDL-64E* used in the experiments.

(b) Dense range measurements colored by distance from the sensor.

Figure 1.2: 3D range sensors measure the distance to the next reflecting object along light rays at several angles. These dense range measurements can also be regarded as a collection of 3D points and constitute the input to the proposed method.

Just recently, sensors providing dense range measurements came up. These are firstly time-of-flight (TOF) cameras, which combine the radiation of infrared light from one light source with standard camera technology to densely measure reflected light [Fra09]. The effective operating distance is limited to approximately 40 meters. Secondly, the integration of several lasers into one housing resulted in 3D lidar sensors, see Figure 1.2(a). Each laser emits a focused light beam in a specific direction, which allows the measurement of reflected light even from distances of more than 100 meters. Since each laser pulse only senses a small part of the environment and the number of lasers in the housing are limited, a sequential measurement process is needed (leading to the term *laser scanner*). This is often accomplished by rotating either a mirror or the whole housing.

This work is targeted at this new class of dense 3D sensors[1]. As illustrated in Figure 1.2, these sensors return range measurements, r, for different horizontal and vertical angles, ψ, θ, which can also be considered points in 3D space, $(x, y, z)^{\mathrm{T}}$. Areas in-between these points are not measured. Hence, these sensors approximate the 3D surface geometry of the environment. One important property is the independence of range measurement imprecision on the measured

---

[1]Although experiments were carried out with a 3D lidar sensor, the use of TOF cameras is in principle possible, too

distance, which stands in contrast to e. g. triangulation based sensors like stereo camera systems. Although many range sensors additionally measure the amount of reflected light, this information is often very noisy and thus not used within this work.

There are several challenges when working with range measurements only. First, it is generally not possible to fully reconstruct the underlying geometry from the 3D points because the sampling theorem [Sha49] is often violated, especially in areas of vegetation. Second, there is no way to identify an underlying object by using one measurement alone. Even if neighboring measurements are taken into account the task remains very difficult since many local surface patches look alike. Third, it is usually impossible to establish exact correspondences between measurements made at different points in time since the measurements derive rarely from exactly the same surface section. Establishing approximate correspondences with the help of neighboring measurements is once more very difficult since many local surface patches look alike. Laser scanners in opposition to TOF cameras bring up one more problem: Each section of the environment is measured at a different point in time. Having the sensor mounted on a mobile platform, leads to a need for a measurement correction based on the sensor motion. Since in this work the sensor motion is inherently estimated, this problem can be compensated for.

1.2   State of the Art

This section gives a brief overview of existing methods that try to solve the afore mentioned perception problems. As it is a wide field of research only the most relevant work is covered, a more exhaustive literature review is given in subsequent chapters.

Though various sensors are available and various problems are discussed in the following, one common distinction can be made: The typically flat surrounding of vehicles allows for some problems to reduce the 3-dimensional (3D) surroundings to a slice-like 2-dimensional (2D) subspace by assuming that the ground can be approximated by a plane and by assuming that all movements occur in parallel to this plane. In consequence, the possible degrees of freedom (DOF) reduce from 6 (3 translations, 3 orientations) to 3 (2 translations, 1 orientation). The advantages are twofold, namely the reduced computational complexity of the algorithms and the increased robustness of the methods. The main disadvantage is that violations to the assumptions may lead to erroneous environment models. This can potentially be lethal when used within autonomous cars.

1.2.1 Localization

The first perception problem is the estimation of the position and orientation, together called *pose*, of the sensor vehicle relative to some reference frame. Among possible reference frames are the road beneath the vehicle, the starting position of the vehicle, or a fixed position on the globe. The availability of the latter is required to use information from roadmaps, which are a common tool for navigation.

The 2D pose with respect to the road can be determined with the help of lane markings. These can be detected with cameras [Dic92, Pin09] or lidar sensors [Lev10]. But missing or misleading markings at construction sites, at intersections, and in side roads cause these approaches to fail regularly.

Other approaches focus on estimating the trajectory of the vehicle relative to the starting point. Here, the quality of the results seems to correlate with the amount of sensor data, which again makes cameras and range sensors suited for this task. Since other moving objects influence sensor data, it is important for these approaches [Bad04, Cam05], also known as *visual odometry*, to either reject outliers [Kit10] or to additionally use wheel speed sensors [Agr06] or inertial sensors [Dor06].

An alternative are techniques for simultaneous localization and mapping (SLAM) [Thr05]. Thereby, the vehicle incrementally builds a map while it moves and localizes itself within that map. The map can have various forms ranging from a sparse collection of features up to a dense set of 3D points. Like visual odometry methods, SLAM methods benefit from dense data, so the choice of sensor is practically limited to cameras, TOF cameras, and laser scanners. Since the latter typically have a large field of view they often give superior localization estimates.

Both, visual odometry and SLAM methods, suffer from drift since errors are accumulated. However, SLAM methods offer the possibility to eliminate accumulated errors when revisiting a place (loop-closure) [Ste10]. The alternative is to use a satellite based global positioning system (GPS) which can be integrated into all the above stated methods. Using GPS alone is in general not precise enough; especially in street canyons multipath effects can result in position errors of more than 10 meters.

All in all, solid algorithms exist for the self-localization of a vehicle. Especially SLAM methods lend themselves to this task due to their precision and possibility to reduce drift through loop-closures. Nevertheless there exists room for improvement. Dense 3D data, as delivered by novel sensors, ask for computationally simpler methods. Especially when localizing with 6 DOF, more data seems to be more important than better algorithms. Additionally, most existing approaches treat moving objects as statistical noise. In public traffic, objects often move in the same direction, distracting the algorithms and leading to a wrong localization. Only a few approaches try to explicitly detect this fault [Wan04, Vu08] and these were only shown to work in 2D.

1.2.2 Detection and Tracking of Moving Objects

The second perception problem is the detection of obstacles, which can also be regarded as the distinction between occupied and free space. When dealing with objects that can move at higher speeds, an explicit detection and tracking of moving objects is required, where *tracking* refers to the process of visually following an object thereby estimating its state. Knowing the state of an object, which commonly includes the position and the velocity, allows the prediction of its position in the nearby future.

The most basic approaches only distinguish between free and occupied space and necessitate the use of range data. By tracing all (light-) rays reaching the sensor, space can be explicitly detected as free up to the measurement point. Storing this information within a 2-dimensional grid leads to the well-established *occupancy grids* [Thr03]. Such grids allow the fusion of sensor readings from various sensors at various positions and points in time by integrating measurements e. g. in a probabilistic fashion. Originally developed for 2D laser scanners, such grids can be used for 3D scanners [Kam08] and stereo cameras [Lat10] too. For the application of autonomous driving, these grids have proven to be an efficient method [Mon08, Urm08, Kam08].

Approaches that explicitly detect and track objects frequently follow the same design, no matter if they are developed for radar sensors, cameras, or range sensors. At each point in time targets are detected in the data, then associated with the detections of the past, and finally used to update the targets' states [BS87]. This *standard tracking pipeline* has been successfully applied to radar sensors in order to track other vehicles [Mar01] and to camera and range data in order to track vehicles or pedestrians [Ess10, Vu08, Mon08, Urm08, Kam08]. Surprisingly, even methods working with dense 3D data track objects in the reduced 2D subdomain only.

The standard tracking pipeline has assets and drawbacks. One asset is the conceptual independence of the tracking stage from the detection stage. This reduces computational complexity and even allows the use of various sensors in parallel. The main drawback is that the detection stage must be reliable and reproducible. For camera and range data this has the consequence that mostly object class specific detectors are used. Hence, when tracking cars and pedestrians only, a cyclist might be overlooked. The few generic detection approaches [Sch08, Far06, Sab96] seem to require the objects to be relatively big and well separated from the background. Both properties are not desirable with respect to autonomous driving. Objects of unknown type as well as smaller objects should be detected and tracked. Another drawback is the update of the state. Nearly all methods track objects by their centroid, which cannot be reliably estimated unless a very precise appearance model is given. This again can only be the case for known object classes.

Another concept is the integration of object tracking into SLAM. This potentially allows the tracking of generic objects as parts of the environment that are inconsistent with the static surroundings. Especially the usage of occupancy grids as SLAM framework allows quick identification of regions that change occupancy. Example implementations were published by Wang [Wan04] and Vu et al. [Vu08]. Unfortunately, their extension to 3D is unclear and the computational efficiency in that case is questionable.

A completely different methodology is *track before detect* [Dav08]. Sensor data is quantized and used directly for tracking and the identification of moving objects is postponed. So-called *stixels* [Pfe10] are one popular example where quantization takes place at fixed image columns. Brechtel et al. [Bre10] propose to quantize the ground plane and to track the cells of an occupancy grid. This does not allow the inference of object relationships but provides an elegant way of predicting the occupancy state of cells into the proximate future – sufficient for most path planning problems. Again, this approach is difficult to transform to 3D.

One step further is the idea to optimize the partitioning of data (which can here be regarded as object detection) and the motion estimation together. However, the proposed solutions [Mic08, Bac10, vdV10] are computationally too complex to be applied in real-time on ordinary computers within the next years.

Hence, all successful object tracking methods are 2D or model based, which requires manual model construction and model selection through classification.

Of the two perception problems, the second is probably the one which needs most further development. Although thousands of publications exist on the topic of tracking, no method seems to offer the possibility to detect and track any kind of object with the full 6 degrees of freedom (DOF) from dense range data.

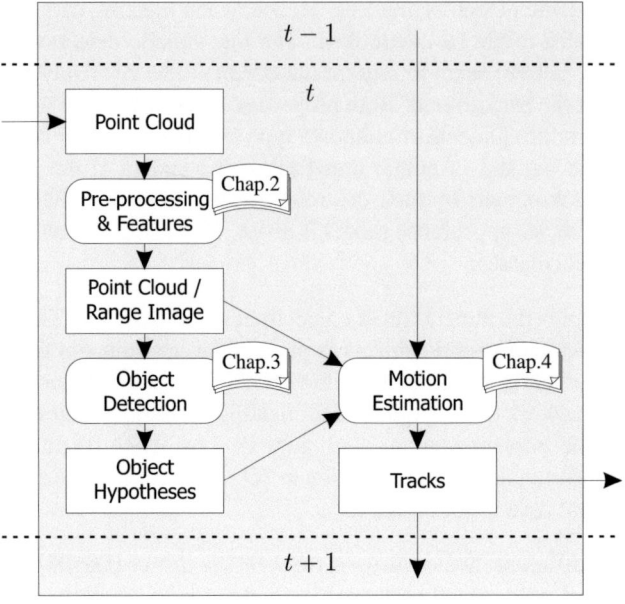

Figure 1.3: Overview of the proposed method. A sequence of point clouds is processed by different stages which are described in the specified chapters. Processing at time t is only dependent on the processing results of the last time step and the input, a set of 3D points. Output is a localization estimate, a set of tracked objects, and appearance point clouds for both, the static world and each moving object.

1.3   Overview

This work proposes a novel approach that integrates localization and object tracking into one common framework. The approach does not assume the surrounding ground to be flat; instead it works in 3D with the full 6 DOF. This is possible by relying on dense and precise distance measurements which can be acquired with the latest sensor technology, e. g. TOF cameras or 3D lidar sensors. The main contributions of this work are twofold:

A novel approach for object detection is proposed that does not use any specific object model. The input data is split into parts with the help of a generic criterion. Hence, any kind of objects ranging from dogs up to trams are detected, see Chapter 2 and Chapter 3.

A novel tracking framework is proposed that resembles the *track before detect* methodology. By taking the detected object hypotheses as data partitioning, a fixed partitioning is overcome, cf. Section 1.2.2. The advantages are an increased adaptability to the current environmental situation and the independence of a detector for specific object classes. Stable results are achieved by accumulating the appearance over time, not only for static objects but for moving objects as well. This so-called *moving object mapping* makes the approach comparable to SLAM methods for localization, but with intrinsically integrated moving object tracking. Details are described in Chapter 4.

Input to the proposed approach is a sequence of dense range measurements only, each being represented by an unordered set of points, also denoted as *point cloud*. No previous knowledge about the environment is needed, neither in terms of a map nor in terms of object models. Output is a 6 DOF trajectory of the sensor and of all moving objects along with an accumulated appearance map in form of a point cloud.

Experiments were carried out on a vehicular platform (Figure 1.1). However, the method is not limited to this application area. In principle, the application to sensor data from flying objects should be possible too. Currently, the sole limitation is the assumption that objects are rigid. Nevertheless, experiments prove the applicability to pedestrians and cyclists.

Figure 1.3 shows an overview of the proposed method. At each time step, the 3D point cloud from the sensor is converted into a range image, preprocessed, and features are calculated, see Chapter 2. Second, each range image is split into parts with each part being a hypothesized object, as described in Chapter 3. After processing each frame independently, motion estimation works by tracking each object hypothesis in 3D over the sequence of data, which is detailed in Chapter 4. A thorough evaluation of the proposed approach is presented in Chapter 5, after which this work is concluded in Chapter 6.

2 Preprocessing and Feature Extraction

This chapter introduces novel ideas for both the enhancement of sensor data obtained at one time instance t and the calculation of distinctive attributes describing local surface patches. These ideas include interpolation and smoothing, the estimation of object borders and the estimation of locally flat surfaces. Additionally, the basic data arrangement and the notation used in subsequent chapters are introduced.

As illustrated in Figure 2.1, the input data at time t is a set of 3D points, $\mathcal{P}_{\mathrm{orig}} = \left\{ (x, y, z)^{\mathrm{T}} \right\}$, also denoted *point cloud*, *scan*, or *frame* in the following[1]. The coordinates are thereby specified relative to a right-handed sensor coordinate system. In case the sensor was a scanning device capturing the data during some small time period, it is assumed that sensor motion has already been corrected for and 3D points are relative to the sensor coordinate system at the beginning of the scan. Correction is possible e. g. with the help of an inertial measurement unit or with the extrapolated motion of the sensor (cf. Section 4.6.2).

Processing 3D point clouds is in general quite time consuming. The unstructured nature of the data especially exacerbates neighbor search. Images, on the contrary, are very attractive, for they implicitly encode neighborhood relations. Since the input point cloud $\mathcal{P}_{\mathrm{orig}}$ dealt with in this chapter was captured from approximately one viewing point, it is possible to transform it into a virtual range image by projecting all 3D points onto the image and storing the distance as pixel values, as illustrated in Figure 2.2 and Figure 2.3. Depending on the type of sensor used, the range image can either have a planar, cylindrical, or spherical shape.

In case the sensor was moving or in case the image resolution is not sufficient, ambiguities can arise from measurements projected to the same pixel. Here, ambiguities are resolved by discarding all measurements but the closest for each pixel. This is not critical with respect to autonomous driving because, firstly, closer obstacles are more relevant than distant obstacles and, secondly, the number of discarded measurements can in practice be kept very low by choosing an appropriate image resolution.

---

[1]The term *point cloud* puts emphasis on the type of data, *scan* on the acquisition spot, and *frame* on the temporal origin.

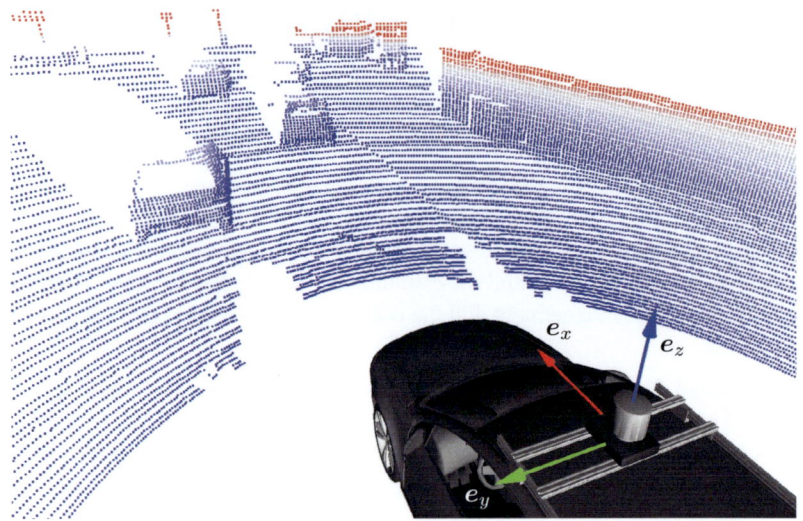

Figure 2.1: Exemplary input data: 3D point cloud captured with a *Velodyne HDL64E* lidar scanner [Sch10] mounted on top of a car. Color encodes the vertical position with respect to the sensor (blue: below the sensor, gray: same level, red: above the sensor). The scene contains a wall on the right and several cars in front of the sensor car which all cast *shadows*, i.e. areas not visible to the scanner.

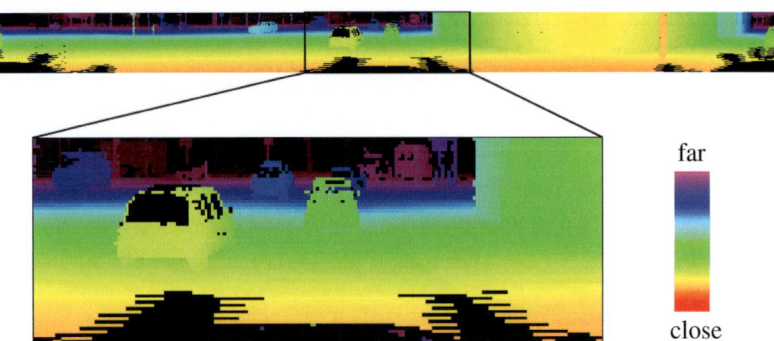

Figure 2.2: Panoramic range image corresponding to one scan. The enlarged part is equivalent to the 3D view shown in Figure 2.1. Pixels contain range values, r_i, which specify the distance from the sensor.

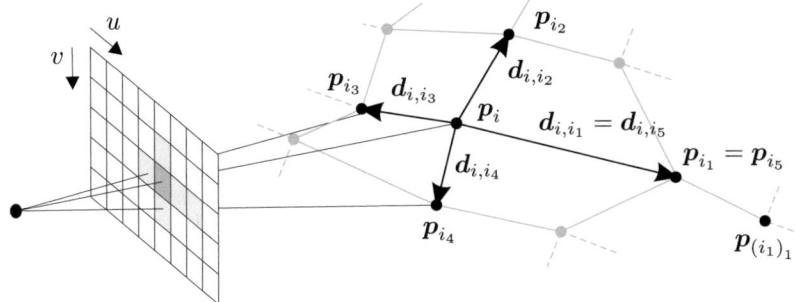

Figure 2.3: A range value in a pixel can be turned into a 3D point using the image geometry and vice versa. Neighbors in the image implicitly define neighborhood relations between the 3D points.

The result of the image projection is an adjusted point cloud $\mathcal{P} = \{\boldsymbol{p}_i\} \subseteq \mathcal{P}_{\text{orig}}$. Since some measurements might be discarded during image projection it is a subset of the original point cloud. Each point of the adjusted point cloud $\boldsymbol{p}_i$ is associated with a pixel (u, v) coding the range value $r_{(u,v)}$. On the contrary, each pixel contains either one point or no measurement at all. This relationship allows replacing pixel coordinates by indices:

$$i \mathrel{\widehat{=}} (u, v)$$

As a consequence, $r_{(u,v)}$ turns into r_i. The advantage of an image-based representation is the possibility to implicitly establish connections from each pixel to its four neighbors. In this work, these are also denoted by indices:

$$
\begin{aligned}
i_1 &\mathrel{\widehat{=}} (u + 1 \ , v \qquad) \\
i_2 &\mathrel{\widehat{=}} (u \qquad , v - 1 \ ) \\
i_3 &\mathrel{\widehat{=}} (u - 1 \ , v \qquad) \\
i_4 &\mathrel{\widehat{=}} (u \qquad , v + 1 \ ) \\
i_5 &\mathrel{\widehat{=}} i_1
\end{aligned}
$$

2.1 State of the Art

Works on preprocessing and feature extraction exist within both domains: the 3D point cloud domain and the 2D range image domain.

The former is frequently an accumulation of several scans and hence has a very equable point distribution. Because of the abstraction from the sensor level, preprocessing of point clouds, especially in terms of noise reduction, is very rare.

Feature extraction, on the contrary, is very common and a good overview can be found in the work of Shapira et al. [Sha09]. The probably most basic and most used feature is a 3D normal vector describing a local surface plane. Various methods evolved for estimating these normals; a comparison is given by Klasing et al. [Kla09a]. Collecting these normals in a histogram can already lead to a good shape description [Ash98]. Especially *Spin Images* [Joh99], a local relative normal vector histogram, are well-known. Lower-dimensional features based on normals also exist, e. g. a feature describing only two points with attached normal vectors [Wah03]. Beside the surface normal vector, the so-called *curvature* [Fly89] plays an important role in literature. It describes the deviation of a surface from a plane. Based thereupon is the so-called *shape index*, which can also be collected within a histogram [Che07]. Apart from these principal features, a variety of other features exist. Mian et al. [Mia06] used e. g. simple point distribution histograms which they call *tensor*. Rusu et al. [Rus09] developed a further histogram representation, the *fast point feature histogram*. Just recently, Makadia et al. [Mak10] came up with a feature describing the silhouette of objects.

Range images correspond to point clouds with implicit neighborhood relations. This allows the just mentioned features to be calculated, too. In addition, this representation allows the calculation of specialized features. Since range images can be interpreted as grayscale images, all features developed in the image processing community can be used. This is especially the case for low-level de-noising techniques like wiener deconvolution [Wie64], bilateral filtering [Tom98], or wavelets [Kov99], but reaches up to higher-level features like the histogram of oriented gradients [Dal05]. However, these techniques are often not optimal because range images have different characteristics. Thus, specialized features were developed. Bellon et al. [Bel99] developed a special method for extracting edges from range images. Lo et al. [Lo09] developed a histogram descriptor inspired by the *scale-invariant feature transform* (SIFT) [Low04], a popular feature descriptor for grayscale images. Novatnack et al. [Nov08] used the image structure to collect tangent mappings in a so-called *exponential map*. Steder et al. [Ste11] showed that explicitly including object borders estimated from a range image improves 3D feature extraction. Just recently, Badino et al. [Bad11] proposed a method that uses the image structure to calculate normals very quickly.

The methods proposed in the following contain basic ideas like bilateral filtering [Tom98], object border estimation [Ste11], and normal vector estimation [Kla09a]. These ideas are adapted to the characteristics of the given data and extended particularly with regard to object detection and tracking – the topics of the subsequent chapters.

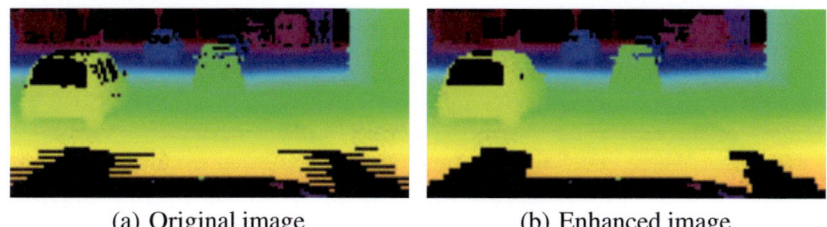

(a) Original image   (b) Enhanced image

Figure 2.4: Result of image enhancement: Gaps are interpolated and values are smoothed. Color encodes distance like in Figure 2.2.

2.2 Image Enhancement

The range images dealt with in this work mainly contain two defects. First, the measured distance is affected by noise. Second, pixels might contain no valid measurement at all if the distance of the target surface exceeds the maximum scanning distance of the sensor. This can also be the case when a specular surface reflects the light. These defects are handled in the following.

The first enhancement step interpolates over missing pixels which serves two purposes. With respect to autonomous driving it is more conservative to assume a measurement (i. e. an obstacle) than no measurement at all. With respect to obtaining good features and segments it is beneficial if all neighbors of a pixel are valid. Interpolation fills gaps first horizontally then vertically in a linear manner, where the maximum gap size is limited to ν_{hPix} and ν_{vPix} pixels respectively and the maximum interpolation step per pixel is ν_{iMax} meters. The values of the three constants allow tuning the method to the given data, see Section 5.1.3.1.

The second enhancement step reduces noise by smoothing the distance values with the help of a four-neighborhood:

$$r_i \leftarrow \left(r_i + \sum_{n=1..4} \mathbf{1}_{I(r_i)}(r_{i_n}) \cdot r_{i_n}\right) / \left(1 + \sum_{n=1..4} \mathbf{1}_{I(r_i)}(r_{i_n})\right)$$

To prevent smoothing over edges, the indicator function $\mathbf{1}$ only activates pixels whose distance is in the interval $I(r_i) = \lfloor r_i - \nu_{sMax}, r_i + \nu_{sMax} \rfloor$. This corresponds to bilateral filtering [Tom98] with the indicator function as similarity kernel.

After enhancing the distance values in the range image, the coordinates of the 3D points are readjusted in correspondence. An exemplary result of image enhancement is depicted in Figure 2.4.

2.3   Estimation of Object Borders

Discontinuities in range values are often a cue to identify object boundaries and in turn to identify pixels belonging together. Here, the so-called *linkage* measure is introduced which codes this information. A connection from pixel i to the neighboring pixel j gets assigned a linkage value $l_{i,j}$ close to 1 if the two pixels are likely to belong to the same object and degrades to 0 the less likely it is.

Pixels are considered to belong together if the absolute change in distance is limited as well as the relative change in distance compared to the connections to the left and to the right. Hence, given four sequential pixels h, i, j, k, the linkage $l_{i,j}$ between the central pixels is dependent on three criteria: the change in distance $(r_i - r_j)$, the change compared to the left neighbor $(r_i - r_j) - (r_h - r_i)$, and the change compared to the right neighbor $(r_i - r_j) - (r_j - r_k)$. Only if all three distances are comparatively low, an object border does not exist.

The linkage value $l_{i,j}$ is obtained by evaluating these three criteria relatively and by combining them in a fuzzy-logical manner [Zad65]:

$$l_{i,j} = \min\{ \text{sigm}(|\tfrac{(r_i-r_j)}{\min\{r_i,r_j\}}| \quad , \nu_{rDiff} \quad , 2/\nu_{rDiff}\ ),$$
$$\text{sigm}(|\tfrac{(r_i-r_j)-(r_h-r_i)}{(r_h-r_i)}| \quad , \nu_{rNDiff} \ , \nu_{rNF}(r_i)\ ), \qquad (2.1)$$
$$\text{sigm}(|\tfrac{(r_i-r_j)-(r_j-r_k)}{(r_j-r_k)}| \quad , \nu_{rNDiff} \ , \nu_{rNF}(r_i)\ )\}$$

The values of the constants ν_{rDiff}, ν_{rNDiff}, and $\nu_{rNF}(r_i)$ are determined in Section 5.1.3.1 and influence the following sigmoid-like function which serves as soft threshold:

$$\text{sigm}(x, \theta, m) = 0.5 - \frac{0.5(x-\theta)m}{\sqrt{1+(x-\theta)^2 m^2}} \qquad (2.2)$$

The value of θ specifies the effective threshold and m is a scale parameter to influence the tangent slope at the threshold, see Figure 2.5.

If $(r_i - r_j) \to 0$ and either $(r_h - r_i) \to 0$ or $(r_j - r_k) \to 0$ a point of singularity is reached. To cover this case, the linkage value is set to 1 in the vicinity of this point. Note that this results in a symmetric measure, i.e. $l_{i,j} = l_{j,i}$. A showcase result is depicted in Figure 2.6.

The idea of explicitly estimating object borders for subsequent feature extraction is also present in the work of Steder et al. [Ste11]. However, Steder et al. work on a larger neighborhood and use operations in 3D and 2D. While this might prove to be more robust in general, it might fail on low resolution images. Additionally, its computational complexity is significantly higher than the complexity of the method proposed in this work.

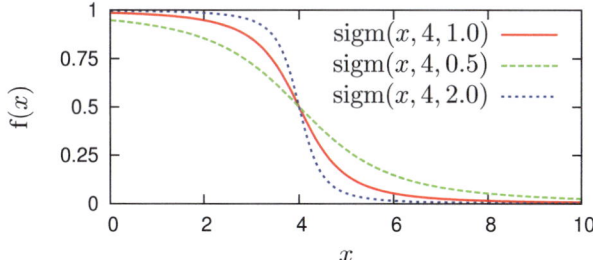

Figure 2.5: The sigmoid-like soft threshold function is used to map arbitrary values to the interval [0,1] and sets the base for fuzzy-logical operations.

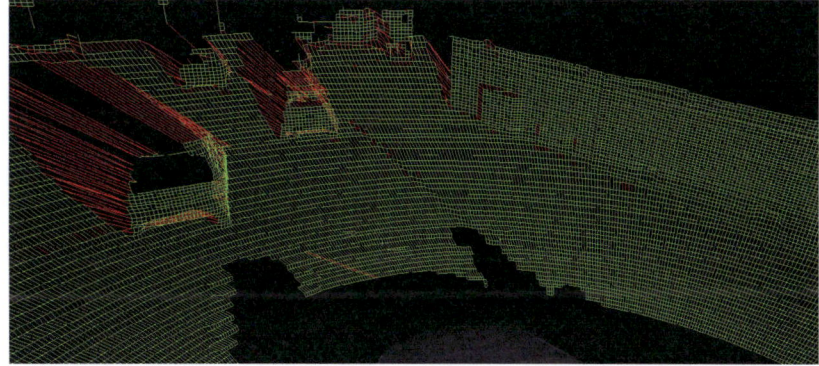

Figure 2.6: Object boundaries can be estimated by comparing neighboring range measurements. The larger the difference is, the more likely it is that the pixels do not belong to the same object which leads to a low linkage value. These values are illustrated for the range image in Figure 2.2 in the perspective view of Figure 2.1. Color encodes linkage strength $l_{i,j}$ from 0 (red) to 1 (green).

2.4 Estimation of Local Surface Planes

Assuming the local surface geometry around a point, p_i, to be planar is very prevalent, as noted in Section 2.1. In the following, an efficient method for calculating the normal vector, n_i, of the local plane is described. In contrast to existing works, the presented method explicitly takes object borders into account.

The last section introduced a linkage measure that estimates for two neighboring points how likely they belong to the same object. In case of a low linkage value this indicates an *object border* for the closer point and a *shadow border* for the farther point, cf. Figure 2.7. For the underlying geometry this implies that the object of the closer point ends or continues to the back, whereas nothing can be inferred for the object of the farther point. This relation is expressed in the non-symmetric border measure:

$$b_{i,j} = \begin{cases} l_{i,j} & \text{if } r_i \geq r_j + \nu_{rSB} \\ \nu_{wOB} & \text{else} \end{cases} \tag{2.3}$$

where ν_{rSB} and ν_{wOB} are constants that are discussed in Section 5.1.3.1. The (low) linkage value is retained for the shadow point but overwritten with a constant high value ν_{wOB} for the border point. Using border values as weights in the following normal calculation makes normal vectors get tilted over the edge at border points only:

$$n_i = \frac{\sum_{j=1}^{4} n'_{i_j}}{\| \sum_{j=1}^{4} n'_{i_j} \|}, \quad n'_i = \sum_{j=1}^{4} b_{i,i_j} b_{i,i_{j+1}} (d_{i,i_j} \times d_{i,i_{j+1}}) \tag{2.4}$$

Hence, the normals are based on the weighted cross products over the four neighbors and smoothed by a moving average filter. An exemplary result is depicted in Figure 2.8(a).

2.4.1 Sampling Theorem Violations

Estimating a local surface plane at a point measurement is only feasible if the sampling theorem is not violated and thus neighboring points belong to the same continuous surface. Unfortunately, there is no way of reliably detecting such a violation. Checking the planarity of the neighborhood can however give a clue about the appropriateness of the surface normal vector. A commonly used criterion is the third eigenvalue of the principal component analysis. Here, a new

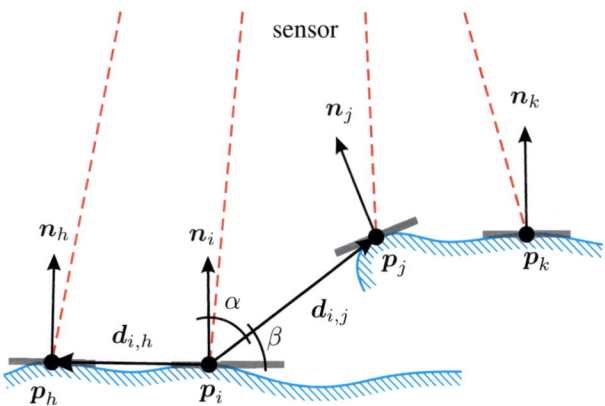

Figure 2.7: 2D illustration of normal vector calculation: The sensor measures the surface (blue) at discrete points (black) from the top according to the light rays (red). Local surface planes (gray) represented by normal vectors are estimated by taking neighboring points into account. Reasoning on the distance measurements allows the detection of the end of a surface (at p_j) where the normal vector gets tilted outwards. For surfaces that become occluded (from p_i to the right) the neighboring measurement (p_j) is not taken into account.

measure is introduced that, from visual examination, seems to produce superior estimates.

As illustrated in Figure 2.7 for the connection from i to j, the angle β of the distance vector $d_{i,j}$ to the plane defines a measure on how likely this connection represents a flat area. This angle can be calculated with the help of α, whose cosine is equal to the dot product between the normalized distance vector, $d_{i,j}/||d_{i,j}||$, and the normal vector, n_i. The flatness measure is defined as:

$$f_{i,j} = \exp\{-\nu_{fDec}\left(\pi - \arccos\left|\left(\frac{d_{i,j}}{||d_{i,j}||}\right)^{\mathrm{T}} n_i\right|\right)^2\} \tag{2.5}$$

where the constant ν_{fDec} controls the decay of the measure. Hence, the measure decays from 1 as the angle β increases.

To obtain the same measure for a point, the values of the four neighboring connections are combined in a fuzzy-logical manner [Zad65]. The plane assumptions at point p_i holds if it either holds horizontally or vertically. However, it is limited by the maximum border value product from the normal calculation:

$$f_i = \min\{\max\{f_{i,i_1} \cdot f_{i,i_3}, f_{i,i_2} \cdot f_{i,i_4}\}, \max_{j=1}^{4} b_{i,i_j} \cdot b_{i,i_{j+1}}\} \tag{2.6}$$

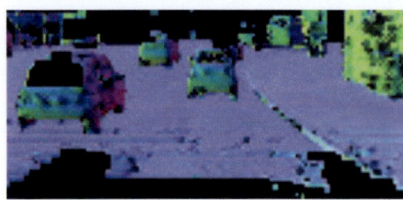 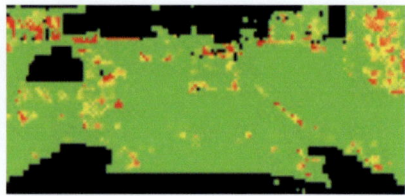

(a) Surface direction, color encodes the direction of the normal n_i.

(b) Flatness values f_i ranging from 0 (red) over 0.5 (yellow) up to 1 (green).

Figure 2.8: Result of feature extraction for the range image in Figure 2.2: For each pixel, a local surface plane is estimated and its adequacy is assessed.

Median filtering is afterwards applied on the 4-neighborhood in order to smooth the values. The result is depicted in Figure 2.8(b) together with the normal vector direction.

3 Object Hypotheses Generation

This chapter aims at identifying regions in the surrounding area that are not necessarily stationary but could move around. Examples include cars, cyclists, pedestrians, dogs, or trams, also summarized by the term *objects* in the following. Such identification of moving objects is a prerequisite for the estimation of their speed and direction of motion, which is in turn crucial for safe autonomous driving.

The aim in this work is to identify for each measurement point p_i the object it belongs to. More formally, the aim is to partition the set of valid pixels[1] $S = \{i\}$ of a frame at time t into segments $S_g \subseteq S$, where each segment corresponds to one object. This is a classical computer vision problem, and according to Gonzalez et al. [Gon92, p. 458] these groups must satisfy:

1. $\bigcup_g S_g = S$

2. $\forall g, h, g \neq h : S_g \cap S_h = \varnothing$

3. $\forall g : S_g$ is a connected region

4. $\forall g : \mathrm{pred}(S_g) = \mathit{true}$

5. $\forall g, h, g \neq h : \mathrm{pred}(S_g \bigcup S_h) = \mathit{false}$

where pred is a predicate over the elements in a set characterizing desired properties like texture or geometrical structure. Exemplary, a predicate could return true if for each normal vector of a segment its difference to the segment's mean normal vector is smaller than some constant angle. The result would be a set of segments with each segment representing a plane.

After reviewing related work, this chapter introduces a novel predicate dubbed *local convexity* and describes an efficient algorithm for employing it.

3.1 State of the Art

Existing works on object detection differ mostly in the definition of the predicate pred and in the algorithm used to apply the predicate. Two groups of approaches

---

[1] Pixels containing no valid range measurement are simply not contained in the set.

can be formed, those using explicit object models and those working with more generic predicates.

The former group is tuned for specific object classes and is best described by the term *object detectors*. Typically, the predicate has a complex global nature and is learned from training images. Examples can mostly be found for intensity images and include support vector machines on feature histograms [Dal05] or voting with shape templates [Fer10]. The employed algorithm usually follows either a hypothesize-and-verify or voting framework where the hypotheses are generated by a rather simple algorithm like testing all rectangular regions of a fixed size at regular intervals [Jur05]. Especially for common "intensity" images these methods achieve amazing results [Uij10], but seem to work for data from 2D laser scanners [Nas08] and 3D laser scanners [Kid11], too. Drawbacks are the high computational complexity, the need for a vast quantity of training examples, the ability to detect only learned object classes, and often the only coarse localization capabilities via bounding boxes[2].

The latter group uses more generic criteria in order to define the predicate. Higher-level semantics are usually ignored and decisions are based on local image regions leading to the simple denomination as *segmentation methods*. Since these methods are potentially fast and able to detect even never-seen object classes, this approach is adapted in this work. The following summarizes the most relevant segmentation methods for range data.

Early works were motivated by industrial applications. Measured objects exhibited flat surfaces, which lead to few noise and prominent edges in the range data. Proposed approaches used these characteristics in various ways. Besl et al. [Bes88] made use of the simple object geometry and segmented by fitting smooth bivariate functions to the data, which automatically handled noise and yielded the segmentation. Hoffman et al. [Hof87] exploited the low noise ratio and grouped pixels with similar curvature, classified the resulting segments and boundaries, and finally merged segments to yield object hypotheses. Han et al. [Han88] focused on the prominent edges, which, after detection, they classified into convex, concave, and jump edges. Regions were afterwards grouped if they were connected by a convex edge. All these methods fail on data captured with today's sensors in outdoor environments, but they nevertheless constitute a solid foundation for modern methods.

Today's outdoor range data is characterized by heavy clutter, complex object geometries (e. g. bicycles), and sometimes even a violated sampling theorem (cf. Section 2.4.1). To avoid especially the latter, some research groups accumulate

---

[2]This makes need for altering the segmentation definition by omitting item 1, item 2, and item 5.

data from various scanning positions to get dense 3D point clouds. This holds especially for air-borne data [Fil02, Dor07], but also for ground-based outdoor data [Nü07] and indoor data [May09]. These huge point clouds are often segmented with fast methods like region growing on similar normal vectors [Rab06], curvature features [Jag07], or region growing of planes [Zav09]. All these methods decide locally about which pixels to merge. A more global view on the segmentation problem provides the ability to revise locally wrong decisions but leads to computationally complex methods. Examples include minimum spanning trees [Agu07] or the watershed cut algorithm [Cou09] for cost graphs. Although inspiring, all these methods are not directly applicable for single-scan data since they rely on a constant point distribution.

Segmentation methods working on single-scan outdoor data are currently all vehicle-based. Since the environment of a vehicle is typically flat and many measurements are on the ground, these methods often perform ground detection first and handle the object segmentation afterwards. This does not only speed up the method but also enables to implement the object segmentation as simple clustering of remaining high-density areas in an artificial 2-dimensional bird eye's view. Examples include the works of Steinhauser et al. [Ste08], Himmelsbach et al. [Him10], and Douillard et al. [Dou11] but also the work of Guo et al. [Guo11] who only focus on ground-obstacle separation. A different approach is taken by Klasing et al. [Kla08, Kla09b] who segment by looking at distance differences and the change of normal vectors. However, the methods were developed for relatively big objects. A similar restriction holds for the works of Sabata et al. [Sab96] and Meier et al. [Mei98], where only big and planar objects can be separated.

All in all, no method seems to exist that was shown to work well for arbitrary objects in a general outdoor setting including hilly environments with vegetation and complex object geometries. This was the motivation to develop the approach presented in the following.

3.2   Local Convexity

The principal idea for forming the segmentation predicate pred is based on the observation that objects are often composed of parts that have a convex shape. Such a shape is commonly referred to as *convex set* [Pre85, p. 18], which means that for any two points within the volume all points on the connecting straight line are also part of the volume. This is exactly the case if the surface is convex at all surface points [Gug63, p. 253]. Convexity of surfaces can e. g. be measured

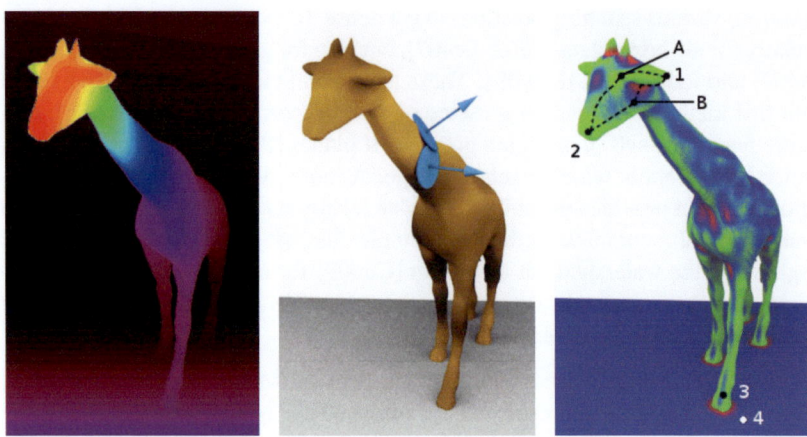

(a) Range image, color encodes distance like in Figure 2.2.

(b) 3D model with two locally estimated surfaces represented by normal vectors.

(c) Local geometry ranging from convex (green) over planar (blue) to concave (red).

Figure 3.1: Many objects have a varying local object geometry. Often, any two points (e. g. 1 and 2 in (c)) on the object can be connected by a path that traverses only convex or flat areas (e. g. A). On the contrary, the transition to another object (e. g. between 3 and 4) usually requires crossing a concave area.

by means of the curvature value, which is positive for a convex geometry, negative for a concave geometry, and zero for flat surfaces, see Figure 3.1(c). The advantage of the surface-based definition is its applicability to range data, which characterizes the surface and not the volume.

For many objects convexity does not hold at all surface points. Take as example the giraffe in Figure 3.1 – an object that is very unlikely to be encountered in urban traffic but that is required to be detected nevertheless. When looking at the mean curvature in Figure 3.1(c), it is clear that e. g. the transition between the ear and the side of the head (transition B) is concave, i. e. it has a negative curvature. Hence, the connecting straight line between the outer ear (point 1) and the jaw (at point B) is not part of the giraffe. However, the upper surface of the ear connects with the forehead (transition A) in a convex manner, i. e. with a positive curvature. Similarly, many other parts of the giraffe are connected by convex surfaces. In contrast, at the transition to another object (e. g. from point 3

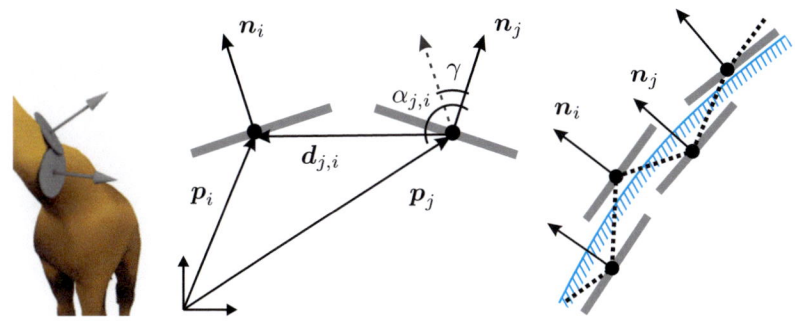

(a) 3D Model (b) In a convex configuration each (c) Measurement noise
with two measurement is below the other can violate the as-
surfaces. surface. sumption of (b).

Figure 3.2: Idea of the proposed segmentation method: Convexity can be evaluated locally by means of the angle between (b) the surface normal and the distance vector and (c) the two surface normals.

to the ground at point 4) the surface is always concave. This observation can be used to define objects as sets of *locally-convex* connected surfaces.

Before putting this idea into action, two factors must be noticed with respect to the data used in this work: First, surfaces are not represented by continuous functions in the 3D space but subsampled at certain points indexed by the image pixels. Second, all measurements are affected by noise. One possible implication is sketched in Figure 3.2(c) where a planar surface turns into a zigzag path. Both factors inhibit the use of curvedness as convexity measure. The main objective is hence to find a new measure defining when two neighboring pixels i, j connect.

The proposed criterion is named *local convexity* and was first introduced in 2009 [Moo09]. In the following, an improved variation is introduced. As depicted in Figure 3.2, the used information consists of 3D point locations, $p_{i/j}$, their relative position, $d_{i,j} = -d_{j,i}$, and an estimate of the local surface planes represented as normal vectors, $n_{i/j}$, pointing outwards.

Several features with increasing complexity are calculated. Their formulation follows the *fuzzy logic* approach where hard decisions are avoided and membership values represent a soft assignment to *true* and *false* [Zad65]. To obtain a good scaling, several constants ν are introduced. Their values are determined in Section 5.1.3.1.

The first feature is a pair-wise characteristic of the surface directions, as sketched in Figure 3.2. Two surfaces are considered *locally convex* if either the surface directions coincide or each point lies below the other surface. This is expressed with the convexity value

$$c_{i,j} = \max \left\{ \begin{array}{l} \mathrm{sigm}(-\boldsymbol{n}_i^\mathrm{T}\boldsymbol{n}_j, -\cos(\nu_{nSim}), \nu_{nSimF}), \\[2ex] \mathrm{sigm}(\max\{\frac{\boldsymbol{n}_i^\mathrm{T}\boldsymbol{d}_{i,j}}{||\boldsymbol{d}_{i,j}||}, \frac{\boldsymbol{n}_j^\mathrm{T}\boldsymbol{d}_{j,i}}{||\boldsymbol{d}_{j,i}||}\}, \cos(90° - \nu_{conv}), \nu_{convF}) \end{array} \right\}$$

$$(3.1)$$

where sigm is the sigmoid-like soft threshold function defined on page 16 by Equation 2.2.

The upper line evaluates the similarity of the surface directions by taking the dot product of the normal vectors, see Figure 3.2(c). The dot product equals the cosine of the angle γ between the vectors, which is 1 for identical normal vectors and degrades to -1 for opposing normals. This angle is compared against a constant similarity angle $\nu_{nSim} > 0$, which can be chosen to account for noisy data, as mentioned above. The negative sign within the sigm function must be used to retain a high value for similar normals, since the sigm function is monotonically decreasing.

The lower line calculates the cosine of the angles $\alpha_{i,j}$ and $\alpha_{j,i}$ between each normal and its distance vector, as illustrated in Figure 3.2(b), which is equal to the normalized dot product. The value is zero if the normal is perpendicular to the distance vector, i. e. if the area is flat. If the other point lies above the surface the value turns positive, if the point lies below the surface the value turns negative – which is the case for convex geometries. By taking the maximum of the two values the most concave (or less convex) configuration is selected. As above, this value is compared against a constant threshold, ν_{conv}, which can be chosen to set the allowed level of concavity (zero = none) as it defines the angle in which the other point may lie above the surface plane.

The constants ν_{convF} and ν_{nSimF} can be varied to set the slope of the sigmoid function at the threshold. As a result, the value $c_{i,j}$ is close to 1 if the two surfaces are *locally convex* and close to 0 otherwise.

Thresholding on such a simple measure can already lead to good segmentations [Moo09]. But the robustness can be improved by taking the surrounding measurements into account. Hence, the second feature extends the first pair-wise feature to triples. A triangle between the measurements i, j, and k is regarded being *triangular convex* if all three pair-wise connections are *locally convex*:

$$c_{i,j,k} = \min\{c_{i,j}, c_{j,k}, c_{i,k}\} \qquad (3.2)$$

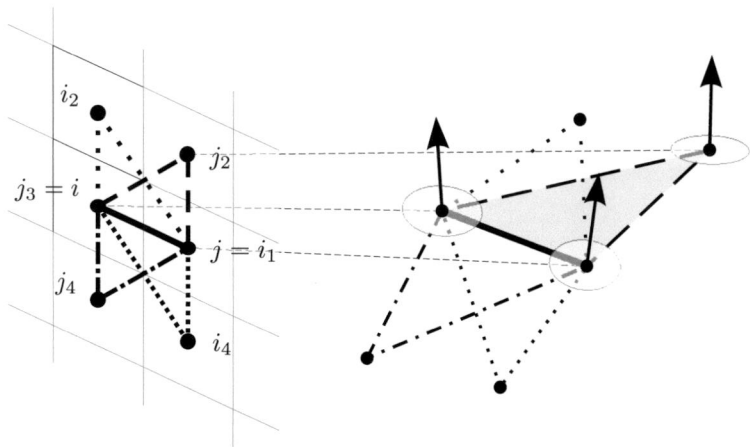

Figure 3.3: The segmentation criterion between neighboring pixels i and j is based on the geometry of adjacent triangles.

The third feature is based upon the *triangular convexity* but returns to pair-wise connections. Figure 3.3 illustrates this feature for a horizontal connection. The so-called *extended convexity* between two measurements i and j holds if any of the adjacent triangles containing these two measurements are *triangular convex*. Mathematically this is expressed by

$$c^{X}_{i,j=i_1} = \max\{c_{i,j,i_2}, c_{i,j,i_4}, c_{i,j,j_2}, c_{i,j,j_4}\} \qquad (3.3)$$

The advantage of *extended convexity* over *local convexity* is constituted by the fact that more measurements are taken into account, which makes the approach more robust to noise. Additionally, a slight twisting of the surface can successfully be detected and suppressed. For an illustration see Figure 3.4.

The extended convexity value $c^{X}_{i,j}$ is finally combined with the linkage value $l_{i,j}$ to form the segmentation decision which is illustrated in Figure 3.5:

$$s_{i,j} = \begin{cases} true & \text{if } c^{X}_{i,j} \cdot l_{i,j} >= \nu_{st} \\ false & \text{else} \end{cases} \qquad (3.4)$$

One important property follows from the above definitions: $s_{i,j} = s_{j,i}$ i. e. the criterion is symmetric. This can easily be verified since all of the features $l_{i,j}$,

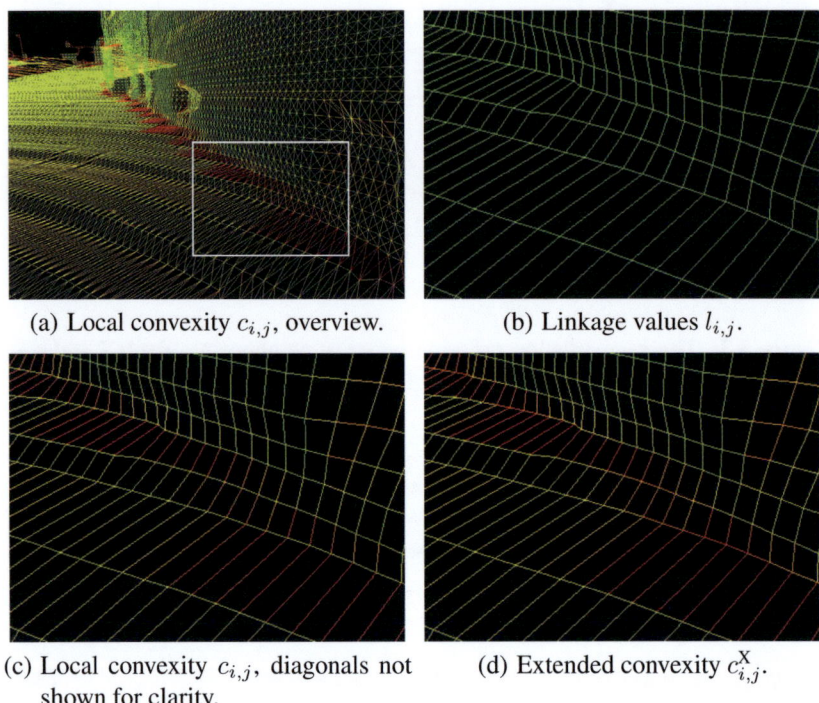

(a) Local convexity $c_{i,j}$, overview.   (b) Linkage values $l_{i,j}$.

(c) Local convexity $c_{i,j}$, diagonals not   (d) Extended convexity $c_{i,j}^{X}$.
    shown for clarity.

Figure 3.4: Criteria used for segmentation illustrated on a zoom-in of the wall in Figure 2.1, values colored from red (0) over yellow (0.5) to green (1). The difference between local convexity and extended convexity can be clearly seen at the horizontal connections in (c) and (d). Local convexity might group the wall and the floor together whereas extended convexity clearly separates the two objects.

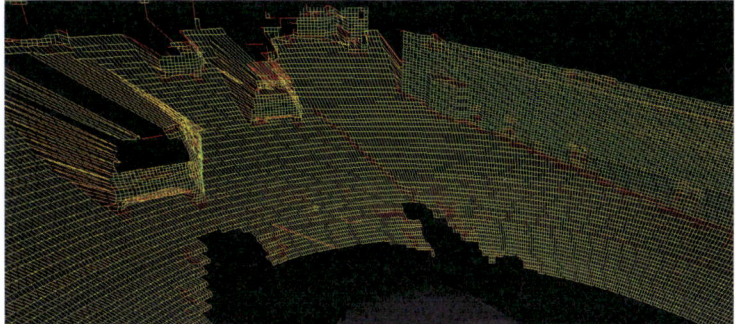

(a) Extended convexity $c_{i,j}^X$ ranging from 0 (red) over 0.5 (yellow) to 1 (green).

(b) Segmentation decisions $s_{j,i}$. White connections indicate grouping of pixels.

(c) Segments $\{S_g\}$, filtered. Each segment is shown in a different color.

Figure 3.5: Using local convexity for segmentation of the scene of Figure 2.6.

$c_{i,j}^{X}$, and $c_{i,j}$ are symmetric. Applying this criterion to the problem of segmentation, this property enables the use of an efficient segmentation algorithm which is described in the next section.

3.3 Segmentation Algorithm

The last section presented a criterion, which decides locally whether neighboring pixels belong together or not. From a global perspective this means that all pixels that are connected by some path belong to the same segment. Vice versa, all elements in a segment $\mathcal{S}_g$ are connected by some path, or, $\mathcal{S}_g$ is a connected set. Hence, the segmentation predicate pred simply verifies whether the given set is connected:

$$\mathrm{pred}(\mathcal{S}_g) = \textit{true} \ \text{ iff } \ \forall i, m \in \mathcal{S}_g \ \exists j, \ldots, l \in \mathcal{S}_g : s_{i,j} \wedge \ldots \wedge s_{l,m} = \textit{true}$$

$$(3.5)$$

The predicate holds if and only if there exists a connected path between any two elements i, m of the set $\mathcal{S}_g$ so that the path is fully contained in the set.

Given the local segmentation decisions $s_{i,j}$, the remaining problem is to cumulate the connected pixels within a data structure representing the segment. In other words, the segment or segment index must be determined for each pixel. This problem is also known as *connected components labeling*. In [Sha01, pp. 69–73] an algorithm is explained that performs the associations between pixels and segments with two passes across the image. In the first pass, a local data structure is built that stores the associations. In the second pass these are propagated back to the pixels. This algorithm is used here. As result, each pixel *knows* the segment it belongs to and each segment keeps a list of the contained pixels.

The above method fulfills all five requirements described at the beginning of this chapter. This is especially true for item 1, which states that the union of all segments is exactly the set of valid pixels. This induces that segments might exist that consist of only one or two pixels. With respect to tracking, such small segments are not desirable since the motion of only a few pixels cannot be reliably estimated. As a consequence, only segments with a sufficient size are accepted as object hypotheses:

$$|\mathcal{S}_g| \geq \nu_{minPix} \qquad\qquad\qquad (3.6)$$

This filtering leads to item 1 of the segmentation definition being violated, but makes the following tracking stage more reliable. Figure 3.5 depicts the result for example data.

Summarizing, this chapter showed how an initial set of pixels S can be turned into groups of disjoint sets $S_g \subseteq S$. Since the pixels derive from range measurements, each group corresponds to a set of points in 3D space and is regarded as an object. The underlying idea for grouping was that most objects have locally convex shapes and that the transition to other objects is usually concave.

4 Motion Estimation

Previous chapters work on data which is obtained at approximately one time instance. Although processing sensed data captured at the current time t is of uttermost importance for autonomous driving, temporal relations are fundamentally necessary since driving is a dynamic process, which is influenced by the past and the predicted proximate future. Consequently, this chapter focuses on sequences of data.

Taking the object hypotheses from the last chapter as a basis, goal of this chapter is to track these objects over time. The term *tracking* refers to the process of visually following an object, thereby estimating its state and hence its motion. The time-dependent state is commonly represented as a vector $x(t)$ comprising the object's position, orientation and their derivatives but can include other variables like shape or appearance as well. The sequence of state vectors, which emerges by tracking an object over time, is commonly named *track*. If multiple objects are tracked at the same time the term *multi target tracking* is used.

Most of the object hypotheses represent stationary objects. By tracking their state with respect to the sensor vehicle, it is possible to deduce the motion of the sensor vehicle with respect to the environment (commonly referred to as *ego motion*) – it is simply the inverse of the motion of stationary objects.

Before the proposed method is explained in detail, related work is pointed out and their relationship to this work is discussed.

4.1 State of the Art

In literature it is common to separate the goal of this work into two topics: The first is the estimation of the motion of surrounding objects and is known as multi target tracking. The second is the estimation of the motion of the vehicle, which can be regarded as a localization problem.

4.1.1 Multi Target Tracking

The problem of (multi target) tracking emerged at the beginning of the 20th century when radar technology was developed and brought into intensive use during the Second World War. Because measurements are noisy and misdetections occur it is desirable to smooth the measurements over time, potentially allowing the estimation of the true internal state of each target.

Several approaches for state estimation – or state filtering – exist. Bayesian filtering is nowadays a common generalization that falls back to older methods like the Kalman filter, the extended Kalman filter, the unscented Kalman filter, or the particle filter depending on the assumptions made. A comprehensive introduction and review on state filtering can be found in the works of Fox et al. [Fox03] or Bar-Shalom et al. [BS02], the former applying it for localization, the latter focusing more on tracking.

State filtering estimates the state of exactly one object. It therefore needs measurements that are used to update the estimated state. Generating these measurements from sensor data is a non-trivial task. Problems arise especially when multiple objects (i.e. targets) are present at the same time. Many works have been published in the last decades that tackle these problems in various ways.

The most prevalent methodology, called *standard tracking pipeline* in the following, is to treat measurement generation and state estimation as being independent, see Section 1.2.2. Having a set of measurements, the remaining problem is to associate these to existing tracks, to create tracks for objects that appear and to delete tracks for objects that disappear. Possible generic solutions are given in the works of Bar-Shalom [BS87] and Cox [Cox93]. One is to consider every possible association and decide after a short period of time which combination was the most appropriate. This so-called multi hypothesis tracking (MHT) has one big drawback: The computational complexity grows exponentially over time. To break this burden, techniques like the joint-probabilistic data association filter or the even faster cheap joint-probabilistic data association filter were proposed. Nevertheless, MHT remains a popular approach since it performs best and since the number of combinations can in practice be kept low when ignoring unlikely associations.

Applying the standard tracking pipeline to dense data like images or range data requires a reliable and repeatable object detection method, as already argued in Section 1.2.2. In consequence, state of the art methods mostly train classifiers for the detection of specific object classes like cars or humans [Wen05, Ess10]. Only a few methods employ generic segmentation methods to detect objects sticking out well from background [Sch08, Far06]. When using dense data, another problem occurs which is less present in the original radar data. The association of measurements can be ambiguous when several detections per object exist. This happens if the object detection method is not repeatable enough or if generic segmentation methods are used. Several solutions have been proposed for that problem. Streller et al. [Str04] use a modified MHT framework. Reuter et al. [Reu09] combine detections by fuzzy segmentation. Douillard et al. [Dou12] propose to directly match segments using a similarity measure. Gate et al. [Gat08] store the appearance in addition to the track state, updating it with every new measurement. This helps especially if the segmentation method sometimes splits an object apart. Babenko et al. [Bab11] propose *multiple instance learning* – a related idea within the domain of images.

Despite these challenges, the standard tracking pipeline has been applied to various kinds of sensors. 2D laser scanners were frequently used for early robotic or automotive applications [Kap07, Vu08, Nas08]. In the "DARPA Urban Challenge" 2007, these sensors were mainly replaced by 3D laser scanners but tracking methods remained similar [Mon08, Urm08, Kam08, Pet09]. The same holds for methods developed for TOF cameras [Sch08, Far06].

A completely different methodology is *track before detect* [Dav08], which stands in contrast to *track after detect* in the standard tracking pipeline. As mentioned in Section 1.2.2, sensor data is quantized e. g. at fixed image columns [Pfe10] or at fixed intervals in the horizontal plane [Bre10]. Although results seem very promising, finding a good grouping of the tracked partitions, which corresponds to the detection, is still an open issue.

4.1.2 Localization

An initial overview of methodologies for the self-localization of vehicles was already given in Section 1.2.1. Here, the review on methods for simultaneous localization and mapping (SLAM) is deepened since these seem to be the most accurate localization methods and since the present work follows their ideas.

A very good introduction to SLAM can be found in [Thr05], which also includes the trends of the last years towards probabilistic techniques. Most of them store the vehicle pose and the map within a combined state vector and use state filtering techniques [Fox03] for the estimation, as e. g. extended Kalman filters [Leo99], unscented Kalman filters [Che06], sparse extended information filters [Thr04], or Rao-blackwellized particle filters [Gri07]. Excellent results were obtained but most of these methods are computationally hard when the number of measurements grows. Not surprisingly, their application concentrated on the use of 2D laser scanners especially within buildings.

Yet, Holz et al. [Hol10] showed just recently that the combination of several heuristics with simple scan-matching yields a fast approach that is nevertheless as accurate as probabilistic methods in 2D. In scan-matching, for each captured point cloud the capturing pose is determined by the optimal fit of the current scan with the current map, also represented as point cloud. Incremental scan-matching then uses the captured point cloud to extend and update the map. The best fit is determined with so-called registration methods [Sal07]. Though methods exist that find the global optimum [Li07], local methods which iteratively refine a given estimate dominate the SLAM literature because they are computationally less complex and because they are usually sufficient. Nearly all SLAM methods are thereby based on the popular Iterative Closest Points (ICP) algorithm [Bes92, Che91].

When focusing on outdoor environments, the use of full 3D data becomes inevitable. The increasing amount of data notably shifts the used method types in favor of scan-matching. To keep device costs low, all current systems scan the 3D volume by turning a sensor in some way. Nüchter et al. [Nü07] stop the vehicle for each scan and do incremental scan-matching. As this is not appropriate for autonomous vehicles, one has to cope for the sensor movement as scanning times cannot be neglected. One such approach was presented [Har08] for a nodding 2D laser scanner. Another approach [Bos09] spins a similar scanner around its center axis and estimates the trajectory during scanning within the scan-matching. A simple but nevertheless accurate alternative for devices scanning perpendicular to the rotation axis was presented in 2011 [Moo11b] and is detailed in Section 4.6.

Most SLAM methods only seek to estimate the motion of the vehicle and usually average out objects with different motion, as e. g. [Bos09, Nü07]. For low outlier ratios these registration methods provide good results. But as they work by aligning subsequent unordered point clouds, a high portion of moving objects might cause these methods to fail. Only a few SLAM methods try to simultaneously detect and track moving objects [Wan04]. Unfortunately, their computational efficiency and robustness for the application in 3D was not yet shown.

4.1.3   Proposed Approach

The approach proposed in this work stands out against existing approaches by several aspects:

- It follows a generic design and works in 3D with six degrees of freedom. Consequently, the approach is neither restricted to any specific type of environment (as e. g. vehicular environments) nor to the type of objects being tracked. The only assumption made is that moving objects are rigid, but violations up to a certain degree can be handled as shown by experiments with pedestrians and cyclists.

- By following the track-before-detect methodology, the approach does not require an object detection method that is repeatable enough to associate detections across frames. The typical fixed partitioning is overcome by using the result of the segmentation method described in the previous chapter. The final selection and combination of tracks is carried out by a novel track management method.

- The presented approach treats ego motion estimation, object tracking, and map building in a unified way. Stationary objects are treated like moving objects and are tracked relative to the sensor vehicle. So-called *moving object mapping* accumulates the appearance of not only the static scene but also of moving objects which helps when objects become partly hidden.

- A special handling of noise within the context of SLAM is introduced. On accumulating object appearance, measurements are adapted in areas of flat surfaces. This not only makes localization or rather tracking more precise (see also May et al. [May09] within the context of TOF cameras), but also enables the built maps to be used later on as 3D models.

4.2 Overview

A sketch of the proposed tracking method is shown in Figure 4.1. To ease notation, the time dependence is in the following denoted by a left superscript $^t\boldsymbol{x} = \boldsymbol{x}(t)$ or omitted if all designators refer to the same point in time.

The input point cloud of time t is preprocessed, features are calculated, and object hypotheses are generated as depicted on the left and described in detail in the last chapters. Each object hypothesis $^t\mathcal{S}$ is turned into a tracklet $^t_t\mathcal{X}$ which contains the state and the appearance of the object. Hence, the set of tracklets $^t_t\mathcal{T} = \{^t_t\mathcal{X}\}$ is created where the left subscript indicates the creation time. These are predicted and updated across three frames by using the unsegmented but preprocessed input point clouds as reference. After three frames, each tracklet is compared with existing tracks and either discarded, merged with an existing track, or kept as new track. When keeping it as new track nothing changes on the data side; the difference between tracklets and tracks is only conceptual: Tracks are tracklets that were verified and that exist for a longer time period. This is also emphasized

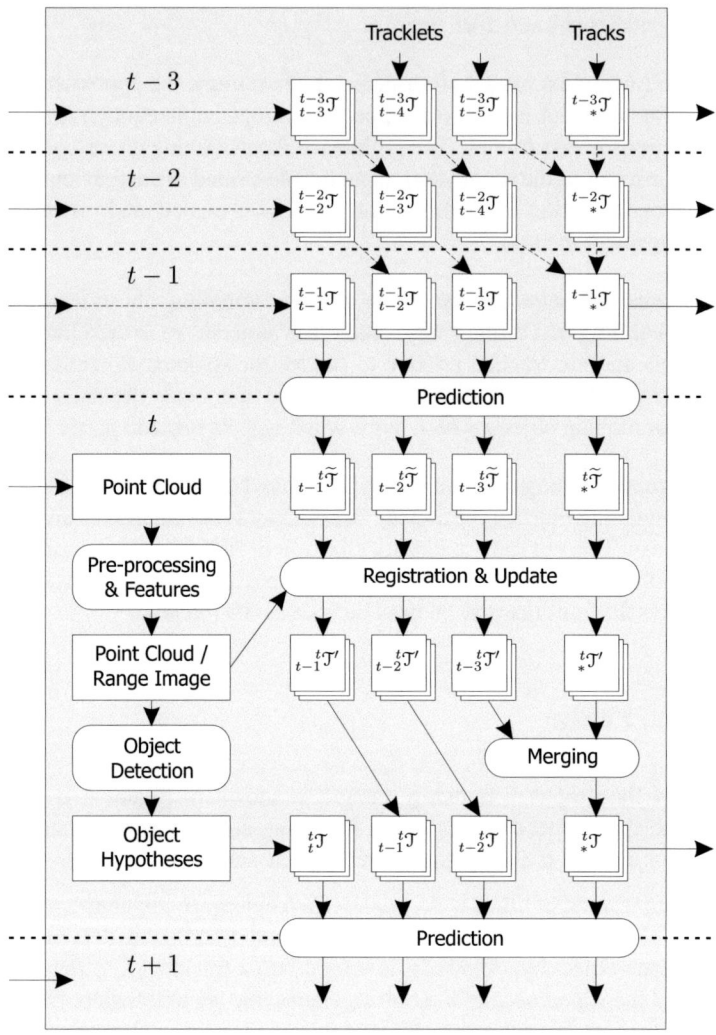

Figure 4.1: Detailed overview of the proposed method. Object hypotheses are tracked over three frames and then merged with existing tracks. Note that the registration step uses the unsegmented point cloud, which is in contrast to most existing tracking methods.

by the notation: The same symbols are used for tracklets and tracks, with tracks $\{{}^t_*\mathfrak{T}\}$ having a mixed creation time.

The details of the whole tracking approach are explained in several steps. The following section details the process of creating, predicting, and updating tracklets. Merging tracklets is the topic of Section 4.4 (merge decisions) and Section 4.5 (merging by *moving object mapping*). Finally, a special handling of the static scene is discussed in Section 4.6.

4.3 Tracklets

The result of the last chapter is a set of object hypotheses, each hypothesis g being represented by a set of pixel indices $\mathcal{S}_g$. This corresponds to a set of 3D points $\mathcal{P}_g = \{p_i \in \mathcal{P} : i \in \mathcal{S}_g\}$ with corresponding normal vectors $\mathcal{N}_g = \{n_i\}$ and flatness values $\mathcal{F}_g = \{f_i\}$. Points and normals are given in the sensor coordinate system S which is indicated by superscript if necessary: $\mathcal{P}_g^S, \mathcal{N}_g^S$.

A tracklet $\mathfrak{T}_g$ is created from the object hypothesis g and can be regarded as object hypothesis in the time domain. A local object coordinate system O_g is introduced, as depicted in Figure 4.2. It is specified by a *pose* vector

$$\boldsymbol{\rho}_g = (\phi, \theta, \psi, x, y, z)^\mathrm{T} \tag{4.1}$$

which defines its orientation and position with respect to the sensor coordinate system using Euler angles[1]. Transformations between the coordinate systems are possible in both directions by applying either the full transformation or only the rotation[2]:

$$\underset{O \leftarrow S}{\mathrm{trans}_{\boldsymbol{\rho}_g}} (\cdot), \underset{S \leftarrow O}{\mathrm{trans}_{\boldsymbol{\rho}_g}} (\cdot), \underset{O \leftarrow S}{\mathrm{rot}_{\boldsymbol{\rho}_g}} (\cdot), \underset{S \leftarrow O}{\mathrm{rot}_{\boldsymbol{\rho}_g}} (\cdot) \tag{4.2}$$

The values of $\boldsymbol{\rho}$ can be initialized arbitrarily. Here, the orientations are set to zero and the position is set equal to a random point from $\mathcal{P}_g^S$. The pose and its derivative constitute the *state* of the tracklet:

$$\boldsymbol{x}_g = \begin{pmatrix} \boldsymbol{\rho}_g \\ \dot{\boldsymbol{\rho}}_g \end{pmatrix} = (\phi, \theta, \psi, x, y, z, \dot{\phi}, \dot{\theta}, \dot{\psi}, \dot{x}, \dot{y}, \dot{z})^\mathrm{T} \tag{4.3}$$

The 3D points, the normals, and the flatness values constitute the *appearance* of the tracklet, which is stored relative to O_g:

$$\mathcal{P}_g^{O_g} = \underset{O \leftarrow S}{\mathrm{trans}_{\boldsymbol{\rho}_g}} (\mathcal{P}_g^S), \quad \mathcal{N}_g^{O_g} = \underset{O \leftarrow S}{\mathrm{rot}_{\boldsymbol{\rho}_g}} (\mathcal{N}_g^S) \tag{4.4}$$

---

[1] Several Euler angle conventions exist, any one can be used as long as it is used consistently.

[2] A possible implementation is discussed in Appendix A.1.

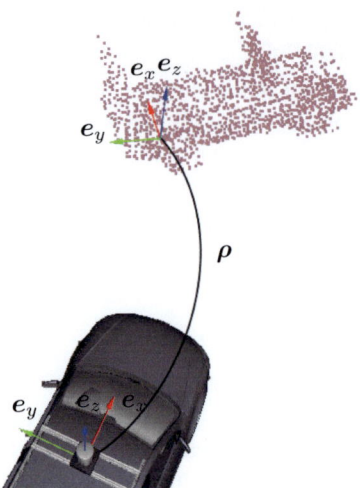

Figure 4.2: Illustration of the state of a track or tracklet (here: a delivery van). The pose ρ of the state vector defines the position and the orientation of a track coordinate system (top) with respect to the scanner coordinate system (bottom). The track appearance is stored as point cloud (violet) with normal vectors and flatness values (both not shown) relative to the track coordinate system.

In total, a tracklet is defined by its state and appearance:

$$\mathfrak{T}_g = (\boldsymbol{x}_g,\ \mathcal{P}_g^{O_g},\ \mathcal{N}_g^{O_g},\ \mathcal{F}_g) \tag{4.5}$$

To indicate when a tracklet was created, a left **sub**script is used. The left **super**script is kept to indicate the current time. Hence, a tracklet at time t that was created one time step before is denoted $_{t-1}^{t}\mathfrak{T}_g$. Note that when the state of a tracklet changes over time, this corresponds to a change of the pose of the object coordinate system O_g, see Figure 4.2. Since the appearance is stored relative to O_g, the whole 3D points and normal vectors "move along" with the object coordinate system.

4.3.1 State Estimation

When an object moves, it continuously changes its state over time. Since the state is defined relative to the sensor, this is even the case for static objects if the sensor moves. In contrast, the appearance of objects does not change over time if objects are rigid – an assumption made in this work. As a consequence, the time-varying state x of a tracklet is continuously estimated by means of state filtering. Possible solutions are usually based on two relationships [Böh08]:

The first relationship is called *motion model* and describes how the state evolves, or changes, over time. In the continuous case this can be expressed by

$$\dot{x}(t) = \mathrm{m_x}(x(t), u(t), v(t)) \tag{4.6}$$

with u being an input signal and v representing model noise. The function $\mathrm{m_x}$ is possibly nonlinear and can include restrictions like gravity or the inability of cars to move sideward. If no input u influences the object, it is called a *static* target because any future state can be predicted by the current state (except for the influence of noise). Otherwise an object is called *maneuvering* target since it might suddenly change its behavior.

The second relationship is called *measurement model* and describes how measurements derive from the state and how they are influenced by sensor noise w:

$$z(t) = \mathrm{m_z}(x(t), w(t)) \tag{4.7}$$

Although the state varies continuously, in this work measurements are made at discrete time steps. Hence, a continuous treatment of the state is discarded in favor of a discrete model. Methods for discretely estimating a state from measurements were already discussed in Section 4.1.1. Here, the Kalman Filter (KF) is selected due to its efficiency. It assumes all quantities to be stochastical with an underlying Gaussian distribution – for the noises v and w with the mean being 0. Additionally, it assumes the models $\mathrm{m_x}$ and $\mathrm{m_z}$ to be linear in the arguments. The result is the linear motion and measurement model:

$$^{t+1}x = M_{xx} \cdot {}^{t}x + M_{xu} \cdot {}^{t}u + M_{xv} \cdot {}^{t}v \tag{4.8}$$
$$^{t}z = M_{zx} \cdot {}^{t}x + {}^{t}w \tag{4.9}$$

When estimating the state of other objects, a possible input u is not known. Thus, it is assumed to be zero ($M_{xu} = 0$) and to be fully represented by the noise term v. Furthermore, the noise is assumed to influence the state directly: $M_{xv} = I$. As a result, the motion model in Equation 4.8 simplifies to

$$^{t+1}x = M_{xx} \cdot {}^{t}x + {}^{t}v \tag{4.10}$$

In this work, generic objects are to be tracked, which prohibits the use of any (possibly nonlinear) restriction. This suggests assuming that each target moves with constant velocity in all 6 degrees-of-freedom (DOF). As a consequence, linearity holds for the motion model of the state ${}^{t}\boldsymbol{x} = (\phi, \theta, \psi, x, y, z, \dot{\phi}, \dot{\theta}, \dot{\psi}, \dot{x}, \dot{y}, \dot{z})^{\mathrm{T}}$ and leads to

$$
\boldsymbol{M}_{xx} =
\begin{pmatrix}
1 & 0 & 0 & 0 & 0 & 0 & \Delta t & 0 & 0 & 0 & 0 & 0 \\
0 & 1 & 0 & 0 & 0 & 0 & 0 & \Delta t & 0 & 0 & 0 & 0 \\
0 & 0 & 1 & 0 & 0 & 0 & 0 & 0 & \Delta t & 0 & 0 & 0 \\
0 & 0 & 0 & 1 & 0 & 0 & 0 & 0 & 0 & \Delta t & 0 & 0 \\
0 & 0 & 0 & 0 & 1 & 0 & 0 & 0 & 0 & 0 & \Delta t & 0 \\
0 & 0 & 0 & 0 & 0 & 1 & 0 & 0 & 0 & 0 & 0 & \Delta t \\
0 & 0 & 0 & 0 & 0 & 0 & 1 & 0 & 0 & 0 & 0 & 0 \\
0 & 0 & 0 & 0 & 0 & 0 & 0 & 1 & 0 & 0 & 0 & 0 \\
0 & 0 & 0 & 0 & 0 & 0 & 0 & 0 & 1 & 0 & 0 & 0 \\
0 & 0 & 0 & 0 & 0 & 0 & 0 & 0 & 0 & 1 & 0 & 0 \\
0 & 0 & 0 & 0 & 0 & 0 & 0 & 0 & 0 & 0 & 1 & 0 \\
0 & 0 & 0 & 0 & 0 & 0 & 0 & 0 & 0 & 0 & 0 & 1
\end{pmatrix}
\tag{4.11}
$$

with Δt being the elapsed time between t and $t+1$.

As explained in Section 4.3.2, the measurement process yields the pose $\boldsymbol{z} = (\phi, \theta, \psi, x, y, z)^{\mathrm{T}}$ of the object. Hence, the measurement matrix becomes

$$
\boldsymbol{M}_{zx} =
\begin{pmatrix}
1 & 0 & 0 & 0 & 0 & 0 & 0 & 0 & 0 & 0 & 0 & 0 \\
0 & 1 & 0 & 0 & 0 & 0 & 0 & 0 & 0 & 0 & 0 & 0 \\
0 & 0 & 1 & 0 & 0 & 0 & 0 & 0 & 0 & 0 & 0 & 0 \\
0 & 0 & 0 & 1 & 0 & 0 & 0 & 0 & 0 & 0 & 0 & 0 \\
0 & 0 & 0 & 0 & 1 & 0 & 0 & 0 & 0 & 0 & 0 & 0 \\
0 & 0 & 0 & 0 & 0 & 1 & 0 & 0 & 0 & 0 & 0 & 0
\end{pmatrix}
\tag{4.12}
$$

Based upon the motion and measurement model, the Kalman filter recursively estimates the optimal state from measurements.

It starts with an initial estimate ${}^{0}\hat{\boldsymbol{x}}$ with covariance ${}^{0}\Sigma^{\boldsymbol{x}}$, initialized when a tracklet is created from the object hypothesis, see Figure 4.1. The initialization of the positional part of ${}^{0}\hat{\boldsymbol{x}}$ was already discussed, its derivatives are initialized with the current negative velocity of the sensor meaning that the object is assumed to stand still with respect to the environment. The covariance ${}^{0}\Sigma^{\boldsymbol{x}}$ is defined by the measurement noise of the sensor (upper left 6×6 matrix) and by the assumed maximum velocity and acceleration of objects. For a more detailed discussion of the initialization see Appendix A.2.

On each further time step, two actions are carried out as sketched in Figure 4.1:

1. The previous state ${}^{t-1}\hat{\boldsymbol{x}}$ is predicted to ${}^{t}\hat{\bar{\boldsymbol{x}}}$ using the motion model (Equation 4.10). The covariance ${}^{t-1}\Sigma^{\boldsymbol{x}}$ is predicted to ${}^{t}\tilde{\Sigma}^{\boldsymbol{x}}$ in correspondence. This step is marked "Prediction".

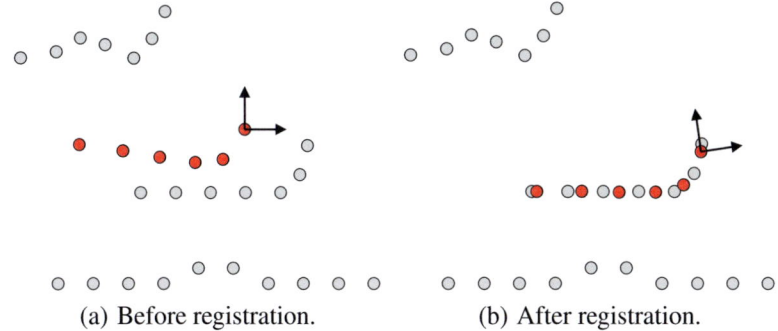

(a) Before registration.   (b) After registration.

Figure 4.3: The measurement for a track or tracklet is generated by aligning the appearance point cloud (red) with the current scan (gray) through minimizing pairwise distances. This results in a modified position and orientation of the coordinate system of the track/tracklet and represents the measurement.

2. The measurement model (Equation 4.9) is used to generate the predicted measurement ${}^{t}\hat{\tilde{z}}, {}^{t}\tilde{\Sigma}^{z}$. This prediction is compared against the real measurement ${}^{t}\tilde{z}, {}^{t}\Sigma^{z}$ and the state is updated based on the difference yielding the new estimate ${}^{t}\hat{x}, {}^{t}\Sigma^{x}$. This step is marked "Registration & Update".

The exact calculations of the prediction and update step are formulated in Appendix A.2. Note that the first step predicts the state into the future based on past observations only. The second step then allows reacting on maneuvers that targets perform which violate the assumption of a constant velocity. However, the second step is skipped if no measurement is available (e. g. in the case that the object is occluded).

4.3.2 Measurement Generation

For the update of a tracklet at time t, a measurement ${}^{t}\hat{z}, {}^{t}\Sigma^{z}$ must be available. As defined by Equation 4.9 and Equation 4.12, the measurement corresponds to the pose $\boldsymbol{\rho} = (\phi, \theta, \psi, x, y, z)^{\mathrm{T}}$ of the tracklet.

The concept of the measurement process is illustrated in Figure 4.3: The appearance of a tracklet is used to align it to the whole point cloud of the current scan. Since the appearance and the object coordinate system O are coupled, a transformation of the appearance automatically results in the same transformation of O, which exactly constitutes the new pose i. e. the measurement. The quality of the alignment can be assessed by the following error function which is dependent on the pose ρ:

$$e_g(\rho) = \sum_{\boldsymbol{p}_i^O \in \mathcal{P}_g^{O_g}} w_i \cdot \mathrm{d}_e^2(\mathrm{trans}_\rho \underset{\mathrm{S}\leftarrow\mathrm{O}}{(\boldsymbol{p}_i^O)}, \underset{\mathcal{P}^{\mathrm{S}}}{\mathrm{nn}}(\mathrm{trans}_\rho \underset{\mathrm{S}\leftarrow\mathrm{O}}{(\boldsymbol{p}_i^O)})) \qquad (4.13)$$

It is a weighted sum of squared distances d_e between the transformed appearance points $\boldsymbol{p}_i$ and their nearest neighbor

$$\underset{\mathcal{P}}{\mathrm{nn}}(\boldsymbol{p}) = \arg\min_{\boldsymbol{p}_j \in \mathcal{P}}\{\mathrm{d}_{\mathrm{nn}}(\boldsymbol{p}, \boldsymbol{p}_j)\} \qquad (4.14)$$

in the sensor point cloud $\mathcal{P}^{\mathrm{S}}$. Commonly, the weights are set to 1 and for both d_e and d_{nn} the 3D Euclidean distance is used [Bes92].

Finding a globally optimal alignment is very complex[3] and thus prohibitive when having a real-time application in mind. The alternative is to optimize only locally, which is sufficient for generating the measurement because the range of maneuvers of an object is limited. A well-established local alignment method is the so-called iterative closest points (ICP) algorithm [Che91, Bes92].

The ICP starts from an initial pose, which is equal to the positional part of the predicted state[4] $\rho_0 = (\boldsymbol{I}_6\boldsymbol{0}_6) \cdot {}^t\hat{\boldsymbol{x}}$. The initial estimate is iteratively refined until a termination criterion is met. The key idea of ICP is to keep at each iteration $k > 0$ the correspondences fixed. This can be expressed by a modified version of Equation 4.13:

$$e_g(\rho_k, \rho_{k-1}) = \sum_{\boldsymbol{p}_i^O \in \mathcal{P}_g^{O_g}} w_i \cdot \mathrm{d}_e^2(\mathrm{trans}_{\rho_k} \underset{\mathrm{S}\leftarrow\mathrm{O}}{(\boldsymbol{p}_i^O)}, \underset{\mathcal{P}^{\mathrm{S}}}{\mathrm{nn}}(\mathrm{trans}_{\rho_{k-1}} \underset{\mathrm{S}\leftarrow\mathrm{O}}{(\boldsymbol{p}_i^O)}))$$

$$(4.15)$$

This error is minimized to yield the updated pose:

$$\rho_k = \arg\min_\rho\{e_g(\rho, \rho_{k-1})\} \qquad (4.16)$$

In the new error definition, the neighborhood assignment nn is dependent on the last pose ρ_{k-1} and is thus fixed during minimization in Equation 4.16. Hence, the

---

[3]The error e is dependent on ρ in two places: in the first argument of d_e and in the argument of nn. The latter is noncontinuous and hence nondifferentiable because neighbor-assignments might change on the slightest modification of ρ.

[4]Using the state as initialization makes the measurement process being dependent on the current state. This violates an assumption of the KF with the consequence of loosing the optimality property. However, many existing tracking methods have a similar dependence, which seems to be necessary when dealing with multiple targets.

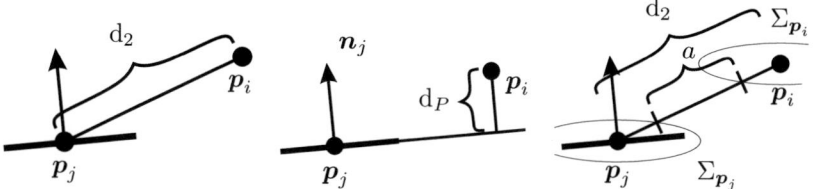

(a) Euclidean distance d_2 (b) Projective distance d_P (c) Mahalanobis distance
(point-to-point).   (point-to-plane). $d_M \mathrel{\widehat{=}} d_2 / (d_2 - a)$.

Figure 4.4: Possible distance functions between two points, used within ICP.

error during minimization is only dependent on ρ in the first argument of d_e. For a common choice of d_e, this modification turns $e(\rho, \rho_{k-1})$ into a continuous, convex function where efficient solvers exist, see Appendix A.3. Determining the correspondences via Equation 4.14 is possible with a so-called *k-d tree*, an efficient search structure if d_{nn} is a Minkowski metric [Ary94].

4.3.2.1 Distance Functions

Several ICP variants have been developed in the past, which all use the Euclidean distance

$$d_2(\boldsymbol{p}_i, \boldsymbol{p}_j) = \left\| \boldsymbol{p}_i - \boldsymbol{p}_j \right\|_2 = \sqrt{(\boldsymbol{p}_i - \boldsymbol{p}_j)^{\mathrm{T}}(\boldsymbol{p}_i - \boldsymbol{p}_j)} \tag{4.17}$$

between 3D points for d_{nn} but vary the employed distance function d_e, see Figure 4.4 for a two-dimensional illustration. The classical variant [Bes92] uses for d_e again the Euclidean distance d_2. The second most frequently used variant [Che91] uses the point-to-plane distance d_P

$$d_P(\boldsymbol{p}_i, \boldsymbol{p}_j) = \left| (\boldsymbol{p}_i - \boldsymbol{p}_j)^{\mathrm{T}} \boldsymbol{n}_j \right| = \sqrt{(\boldsymbol{p}_i - \boldsymbol{p}_j)^{\mathrm{T}} \boldsymbol{n}_j \cdot \boldsymbol{n}_j^{\mathrm{T}}(\boldsymbol{p}_i - \boldsymbol{p}_j)} \tag{4.18}$$

where $\boldsymbol{n}_j$ is the normal vector at $\boldsymbol{p}_j$. Hence, d_P measures the distance of $\boldsymbol{p}_i$ to the surface plane represented by $\boldsymbol{p}_j$ and $\boldsymbol{n}_j$. Just recently, a generalization was developed [Seg09] using the Mahalanobis distance d_M:

$$d_M(\boldsymbol{p}_i, \boldsymbol{p}_j) = \sqrt{(\boldsymbol{p}_i - \boldsymbol{p}_j)^{\mathrm{T}}(\Sigma_{\boldsymbol{p}_i} + \Sigma_{\boldsymbol{p}_j})^{-1}(\boldsymbol{p}_i - \boldsymbol{p}_j)} \tag{4.19}$$

$\Sigma_{\boldsymbol{p}_i}$ and $\Sigma_{\boldsymbol{p}_j}$ are the covariance matrices of a normal distribution representing the local surface shape around $\boldsymbol{p}_i$ and $\boldsymbol{p}_j$ respectively. As visible when comparing the terms under the square root and as discussed by Segal et al. [Seg09], the third variant falls back to the first two variants for an appropriate choice of Σ_{p_i} and Σ_{p_j}.

All three variants have advantages and disadvantages. The first variant is most generic since it does not use any local surface geometry. The availability of a closed-form solver allows significant rotations to be estimated correctly. However, it often returns the wrong estimate for flat objects. Additionally, convergence is slow albeit it is guaranteed to converge. The second version converges very quickly for objects with smooth surfaces. But vegetation and significant rotations pose a problem since the solver needs to linearize the problem. The third variant has the same linearization problem as the second and has much longer execution times. Although it seems to be more robust than either of the other two variants, it does not allow the usage of the calculated normal vectors and flatness values in a straight-forward manner. This drawback makes it less precise than the following adaptive combination of the first two variants, which is equally robust but faster.

The adaptive variant proposed here is based on the average flatness value

$$\overline{f}_g = \frac{1}{|\mathcal{F}_g|} \sum_{f_i \in \mathcal{F}_g} f_i \tag{4.20}$$

of a tracklet. Depending on this value, either of the two variants is selected:

- If $\overline{f}_g < \nu_{ptpl}$, i. e. if the surfaces of the tracklet are not sufficiently smooth, then for both d_e and d_{nn} the Euclidean distance d_2 on 3D point locations is used, as in [Bes92].

- If $\overline{f}_g \geq \nu_{ptpl}$, then the projective distance d_P is used for d_e as in [Che91] but for d_{nn} the Euclidean distance d_2 on 6D point+normal coordinates is used. The latter offers the following advantage: If a point is significantly translated, the original point is still closer in 6D space than a point which is closer in 3D but has a different normal vector. This yields a wider convergence basin for the ICP.

4.3.2.2 Weighting

The weights in Equation 4.15 enable an elegant way of adding uncertainty of correspondences. In fact, if the Mahalanobis distance of Equation 4.19 is used as d_e and if the point distributions are characterized by a diagonal covariance $\Sigma = \sigma^2 I$, the error reduces to the Euclidean error of Equation 4.17 with the weight

$w = \frac{1}{\sigma^2}$. In addition, weights allow the combination of other heuristics like soft outlier detection. As discussed by Holz et al. [Hol10], these may contribute measurably to the precision and robustness of the approach.

This work uses a combined weight $w_i = w_{i,1} \cdot w_{i,2} \cdot w_{i,3}$. For easier notation let

$$d_i = \left\| \text{trans}_{\rho_{k-1} \atop S \leftarrow O} \left(\boldsymbol{p}_i^O \right) - \underset{\mathcal{P}S}{\text{nn}} \left(\text{trans}_{\rho_{k-1} \atop S \leftarrow O} \left(\boldsymbol{p}_i^O \right) \right) \right\| \tag{4.21}$$

be the distance of a transformed appearance point to its nearest neighbor in the scan. Furthermore, let

$$\Upsilon : \mathbb{N} \to \mathbb{N} \tag{4.22}$$

be a bijective mapping on indices that returns for a point index i the index j in the sequence of points sorted by their neighbor distance:

$$i \mapsto \Upsilon(i) =: j, \quad \forall j : d_{\Upsilon^{-1}(j)} < d_{\Upsilon^{-1}(j+1)} \tag{4.23}$$

The first weight $w_{i,1}$ makes the approach robust to outliers. It disables a certain percentage of the correspondences which are regarded as outliers due to a high neighbor distance:

$$w_{i,1} = \begin{cases} 1 & \text{if } \Upsilon(i) < 0.9 \cdot \left| \mathcal{P}_g^{O_g} \right| \\ 0 & \text{else} \end{cases} \tag{4.24}$$

The second weight $w_{i,2}$ softly weights the correspondences by their neighbor distance with the help of a normalizing constant ν_{dMax}:

$$w_{i,2} = \exp\left(-\frac{d_i}{\nu_{dMax}} \right) \tag{4.25}$$

The third weight $w_{i,3}$ prevents occluded objects from being pulled towards the visible area. Therefore, the transformed appearance point is projected onto the image and its distance from the scanner is compared with the distance value at the projected pixel:

$$w_{i,3} = \begin{cases} 1 & \text{if } \text{trans}_{\rho_{k-1} \atop S \leftarrow O} \left(\boldsymbol{p}_i^O \right) \text{ is visible} \\ 0 & \text{else} \end{cases} \tag{4.26}$$

The sum of the weights $w_{sum} = \sum_i w_i$ is an indicator about how reliable the estimated transformation will be because too few good correspondences will lead to a low w_{sum} and to an unstable transformation. Hence, the measurement is only accepted if w_{sum} exceeds a constant minimum weight ν_{wMin}. In particular, this is only the case if enough model points are visible (cf. $w_{i,3}$), i.e. if the object is not largely occluded.

4.3.2.3 Termination

The ICP is an iterative algorithm which needs a criterion for termination. This needs to be robust, since convergence of the ICP is only guaranteed in the variant of [Bes92] and without weights $w_{i,1}$ and $w_{i,3}$, which is not the use case in this work.

The criterion used here is based on the distance of correspondences in Equation 4.21. The weighted average distance at iteration k is calculated using the transformation from $k - 1$.

$$\overline{\mathrm{d}}_k = \frac{1}{w_{sum}} \sum_i w_i \cdot \mathrm{d}_i \tag{4.27}$$

The change in distance $\Delta\overline{\mathrm{d}}_k$ is calculated in a normalized manner as

$$\Delta\overline{\mathrm{d}}_k = \left| \frac{\overline{\mathrm{d}}_{k-1} - \overline{\mathrm{d}}_k}{\overline{\mathrm{d}}_{k-1} + \overline{\mathrm{d}}_k} \right| \tag{4.28}$$

The ICP is terminated if either a maximum number of iterations were carried out, or, if after a minimum number of iterations, the distance change was three times consecutively below a threshold:

$$\begin{aligned} \mathrm{term}(k) = {}& [k \geq \nu_{itMax}] \vee [(k < \nu_{itMin}) \\ & \wedge (\Delta\overline{\mathrm{d}}_k < \nu_\Delta) \wedge (\Delta\overline{\mathrm{d}}_{k-1} < \nu_\Delta) \wedge (\Delta\overline{\mathrm{d}}_{k-2} < \nu_\Delta)] \end{aligned} \tag{4.29}$$

Since ICP optimizes locally, the true solution might not be discovered but instead another local minimum. Robust detection of this case is nearly impossible by using local information (and hence a fast algorithm) alone. As a consequence, existing works typically assume a correct converge of the ICP [Cen07a]. Though this assumption usually holds when matching large point clouds, it is sometimes violated when tracking smaller objects. Hence, this work explicitly detects wrong convergence as follows.

The detection is carried out after the termination of the ICP at iteration k and is based on the Mahalanobis distance

$$\mathrm{d}_M(\hat{z}, \hat{\bar{z}}) = \sqrt{(\hat{z} - \hat{\bar{z}})^{\mathrm{T}} (\tilde{\Sigma}^z)^{-1} (\hat{z} - \hat{\bar{z}})} \tag{4.30}$$

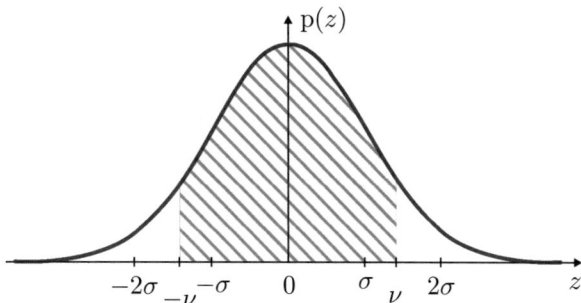

Figure 4.5: Normal distribution $p(z) \sim \mathcal{N}(0, \sigma)$. The area as fraction of the total area corresponds to the probability that a point sampled from the distribution is in the limiting interval $[-\nu, \nu]$. This can be used to reject unlikely measurements which are outside the interval.

between the measurement $\hat{z} = \rho_k$ and the predicted measurement $\hat{\tilde{z}}$ with covariance $\tilde{\Sigma}^z$. Wrong convergence is detected if the distance is above some threshold:

$$d_M(\hat{z}, \hat{\tilde{z}}) > \nu_{dz} \qquad (4.31)$$

An appropriate threshold ν_{dz} can be derived by the properties of the expected measurement distribution $p(z) \sim \mathcal{N}(\hat{\tilde{z}}, \tilde{\Sigma}^z)$. As illustrated in Figure 4.5, the probability that a random sample from $p(z)$ has a distance $d_M \leq \nu_{dz}$ is

$$P_{\hat{\tilde{z}}}(d_M(z, \hat{\tilde{z}}) \leq \nu_{dz}) = \int_{\mathcal{Z}} p(z) \, dz, \ \mathcal{Z} = \left\{ z : d_M(z, \hat{\tilde{z}}) < \nu_{dz} \right\} \qquad (4.32)$$

Hence, choosing ν_{dz} corresponds to choosing a sampling probability. Choosing for example $\nu_{dz} = 1$ equals to choosing the standard deviation, characterized by $\tilde{\Sigma}^z$, as limit which corresponds to a sampling probability of 0.68; choosing $\nu_{dz} = 2$ corresponds to a probability of 0.95.

If the distance of the measurement is above the threshold, i. e. if the measurement in unlikely, the measurement is discarded and the track is left at the predicted state.

4.3.2.4 Measurement Uncertainty

As noted at the beginning of Section 4.3.2, a measurement consists of a mean $^t\hat{z}$ and a covariance matrix $^t\Sigma^z$. According to Equation 4.12 and Equation 4.16, the mean is determined by the pose at the last iteration of the ICP algorithm $^t\hat{z} = \rho_k$, which is the solution of a minimization problem. Possible solvers are detailed in Appendix A.3.

Not discussed yet is the characterization of the uncertainty of the solution in form of a covariance matrix $^t\Sigma^z$. Several sources of error exist, which are all factors for the uncertainty of the estimation:

- Wrong convergence. This source of error was discussed in Section 4.3.2.3. In this work, correct or wrong convergence does not influence the covariance matrix. Instead, unlikely measurements are discarded.

- Underconstrained situation. Such a situation can happen if either too few correspondences are used or if the object shape is symmetric, like e. g. for a disc where the rotation parameter can be chosen arbitrarily. The former case is prevented by ensuring a minimum object size, see Equation 3.6. The latter case can be explicitly detected [Cen07b], but is covered to a large part by the covariance estimation described in the following and by the design of track management in Section 4.4.

- Sensor noise. This is the principle source of influence handled in literature and also the focus in this work.

Several solutions have been proposed, a well-arranged overview can be found in [Cen07a]. The most accurate closed form solution seems to be

$$\Sigma^z = \left(\frac{\partial^2 e}{\partial z^2}\right)^{-1} \left(\frac{\partial^2 e}{\partial w \partial z}\right) \Sigma^w \left(\frac{\partial^2 e}{\partial w \partial z}\right)^{T} \left(\frac{\partial^2 e}{\partial z^2}\right)^{-1} \tag{4.33}$$

which assumes that $\hat{z}$ is the result of an algorithm minimizing an error function e, which has zero gradient at $\hat{z}$, i. e. minimization converged. The vector w represents all input data used in the error function that is subject to noise. In this work it can be regarded as a huge vector with all appearance points, appearance normals, scan points, and scan normals stacked together. Despite the huge size of Σ^w, Equation 4.33 can be evaluated efficiently: Assuming the single point measurements to be independent turns Σ^w into a block-diagonal form. Together with e being a sum, calculation decouples for the single correspondences, reducing the matrix sizes and allowing the calculation to be carried out in parallel.

4.4 From Tracklets to Tracks

Tracklets can be regarded as moving object hypotheses. As explained in Section 4.1.3 and illustrated in Figure 4.1, they are created from (static) object hypotheses and tracked over three frames to check for consistent motion[5].

Since in this work objects are tracked with respect to the sensor, the tracking of stationary objects implicitly estimates the motion of the sensor car with respect to the environment. To improve the quality of ego motion estimation, the very first frame is treated specially: Object hypotheses generation is skipped and only one single tracklet $_0\mathfrak{T}$ is generated that is composed of all measurement points of that frame. As this results in an appearance point cloud which is comprised of surfaces pointing into various directions, the measurement step carried out by ICP is much more robust to noise and hence more precise. Although the generation of this so-called "static" tracklet is specific, the handling in the tracking process is equal to those of "normal" tracklets.

Tracks, as opposed to tracklets, can be seen as output of the algorithm. They are tracklets that have been verified across three frames and they all represent objects moving in a unique way. Hence, they include the static track as one big object moving in a unique way with respect to the sensor. Handling the verification and changeover from tracklets to tracks is the task of a so-called *track management* system, which is marked *Merging* in Figure 4.1 and which is described in the following.

In this work, track management at time t consists of two tasks. The first task is to decide about existing tracks $_*^t\mathfrak{T}_g' \in {_*^t}\mathfrak{T}'$: Either tracking is to be continued or to be terminated, e. g. when the track moves out of the field of view. The second task is to decide about tracklets $_{t-3}^{t}\mathfrak{T}_g' \in {_{t-3}^{t}}\mathfrak{T}'$ which were verified over three frames. Three cases can occur:

1. The tracklet $_{t-3}^{t}\mathfrak{T}_g'$ was successfully verified and represents an object which has a different motion than all existing tracks, including the static track. Hence, the tracklet is to be kept and added to the set of tracks $_*^t\mathfrak{T}'$.

2. A track on the same object already exists. Hence, the tracklet is to be merged with the existing track. Details of merging are described in Section 4.5.

3. No corresponding track can be determined (similar to 1) but the tracklet was not successfully verified. Hence, the tracklet is to be discarded.

---

[5]Note that three frames are required at minimum: The first to get the object position, the second to estimate the velocity, and the third to verify the velocity (or motion)

In all three cases, tracklets are inherently associated and compared with existing tracks. In order to limit the computational complexity, it is desirable that tracklets are associated only to nearby tracks. This association step is detailed next. Thereafter, a method to decide upon the three cases and a criterion for track termination is described.

4.4.1 Tracklet Association

Associations are established at the time of tracklet creation. According to Figure 4.1, there are three existing sets of tracks and tracklets when the tracklets $_{t-3}^{t-3}\mathcal{T}$ are created: the sets of tracklets created from the last two frames, $_{t-4}^{t-3}\mathcal{T}$ and $_{t-5}^{t-3}\mathcal{T}$, and the set of tracks $_{*}^{t-3}\mathcal{T}$. For each of these sets, in the following generalized by the designator $_{-}^{t-3}\mathcal{T}$ and simply termed *tracklets*, associations are established independently.

Given a set of tracklets $_{-}^{t-3}\mathcal{T}$, a virtual range image is generated by projecting the appearance point cloud of each tracklet $_{-}^{t-3}\mathcal{X}_g$ onto that image and retaining at each pixel the closest measurement. The tracklet corresponding to the closest measurement is stored within each pixel and empty pixels are filled with the tracklet giving a majority vote out of the four neighboring pixels, see Figure 4.6(c) and Figure 4.6(d) for an illustration. The projected tracklets are overlaid with the generated tracklets and the association between two tracklets is equal to the number of pixels they have in common, see Figure 4.7. These associations between the tracklets $_{t-3}^{t-3}\mathcal{T}$ and a set of tracklets $_{-}^{t-3}\mathcal{T}$ can be represented by an association matrix

$$_{t-3,-}^{t-3}\boldsymbol{A} \in \mathbb{N}^{|_{t-3}^{t-3}\mathcal{T}| \times |_{-}^{t-3}\mathcal{T}|} \tag{4.34}$$

containing the number of common pixels for each combination. Apparently, $\sum a_{i,j} \in \boldsymbol{A}$ must be smaller than or equal to the total number of pixels.

Track management processes the set of tracklets $_{t-3}^{t-3}\mathcal{T}$ three frames later in the state $_{t-3}^{t}\mathcal{T}'$. In the meantime, track management is applied to $_{t-4}\mathcal{T}$ and $_{t-5}\mathcal{T}$, which are both integrated into the set of tracks $_{*}\mathcal{T}$. Accordingly, the three association matrices $_{t-3,t-4}^{t-3}\boldsymbol{A}$, $_{t-3,t-5}^{t-3}\boldsymbol{A}$, and $_{t-3,*}^{t-3}\boldsymbol{A}$ for $_{t-3}^{t-3}\mathcal{T}$ are merged dependent on the decision taken for each tracklet:

1. The tracklet is kept, i. e. a new track is added to the set of tracks. The according column in $_{t-3,t-4}\boldsymbol{A}$ or $_{t-3,t-5}\boldsymbol{A}$ is appended to $_{t-3,*}\boldsymbol{A}$.

2. The tracklet is merged with one existing track in $_{*}\mathcal{T}$. Employing the idea that the maximal association is the most descriptive, the values in the corresponding column of $_{t-3,*}\boldsymbol{A}$ are overwritten by larger values.

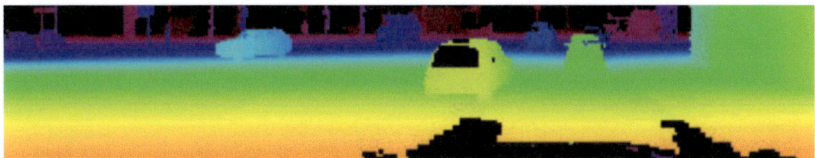

(a) Section of the range image of time t, colored by distance like in Figure 2.2.

(b) Section of the segmented range image, i. e. object hypotheses, corresponding to the tracklets ${}^{t}_{t}\mathcal{T}$ generated at time t.

(c) Tracklets ${}^{t}_{t-1}\mathcal{T}$ that were generated at the last time step projected to a virtual range image at the current time t.

(d) The projection of the tracklets ${}^{t}_{t-1}\mathcal{T}$ can be extended by filling empty pixels based on neighboring pixels.

(e) Extended projection of the tracks ${}^{t}_{*}\mathcal{T}$ which comprise the static scene and all objects detected as moving.

Figure 4.6: Track and tracklet projection.

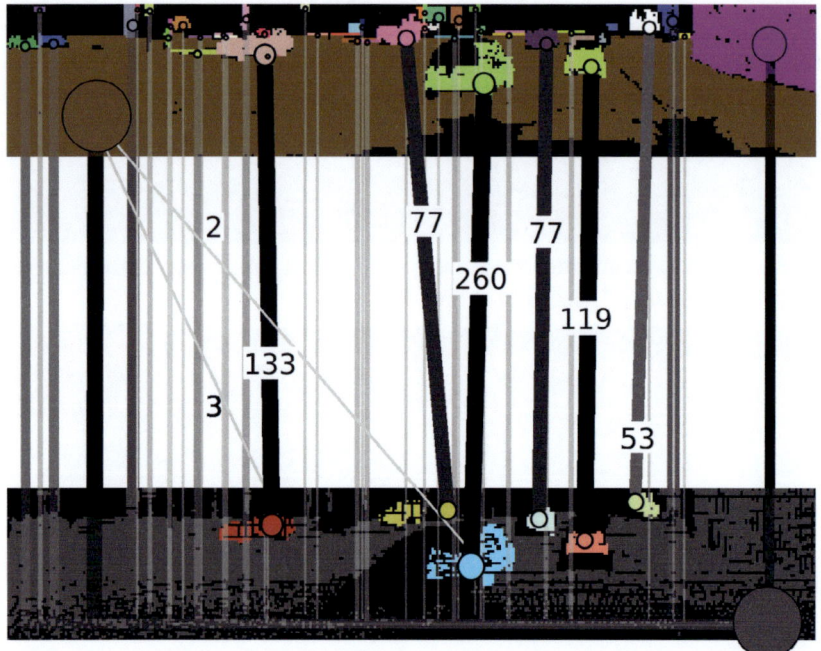

Figure 4.7: Associations between new tracklets ${}_{t}^{t}\mathcal{T}$ (upper image) and tracks ${}_{*}^{t}\mathcal{T}$ (lower image) are established by overlaying their projections, i. e. Figure 4.6(b) and Figure 4.6(e), and counting the number of pixels they overlap. These associations can be interpreted as a graph with edge strengths corresponding to the amount of overlap. Shown are the edge strengths for the associations with moving objects (in the lower figure); the edges that are not labeled are associations with the static track (gray). An association graph is also build between the new tracklets ${}_{t}^{t}\mathcal{T}$ and the tracklets generated from the last two frames, ${}_{t-1}^{t}\mathcal{T}$ and ${}_{t-2}^{t}\mathcal{T}$ (not shown).

3. The tracklet is ignored. Since $_*\mathcal{T}$ is not altered $_{t-3,*}A$ is not altered either.

The resulting matrix $_{t-3,*}^{t}A$ captures all associations from the tracklets $_{t-3}^{t}\mathcal{T}'$ to tracks $_*^{t}\mathcal{T}'$ used in the decision step, which is described next.

4.4.2 Decision Making

Using again the notation of Figure 4.1, for each tracklet $_{t-3}^{t}\mathcal{T}'_g \in {}_{t-3}^{t}\mathcal{T}'$ a decision is made independently about the three cases with the help of the association matrix $_{t-3,*}^{t}A$. The entries $a_{g,h} \in {}_{t-3,*}^{t}A$ thereby characterize for each tracklet $_{t-3}^{t}\mathcal{T}'_g$ the strength of the association to track $_*^{t}\mathcal{T}'_h$.

Making a decision about one of several cases is also known as classification problem [Dud01]. Algorithms for classification typically take a feature vector f as input and output the most likely class, which corresponds to the decision. Important for a good performance is a feature vector that is descriptive enough so that the different classes are well-separated in feature space. In this work, a tracklet $_{t-3}^{t}\mathcal{T}'_g$ is characterized by a 52-dimensional feature vector f_g that captures whether the motion estimated for the tracklet during the last frames is reasonable and whether the motion of an existing, associated track also fits for the tracklet. A detailed listing of the entries of f_g is given in Appendix A.4.1, a comprehensive explanation is given in the following.

The detection of unreasonable motion was partly covered by the rejection of measurements in Equation 4.32. However, slight inconsistencies in the beginning are not rejected because the state covariance is initialized with high values. Furthermore, unreliable motion estimation is hardly discovered: As illustrated in Figure 4.8(b), a flat object can be moved along e. g. a wall and both, the point-to-point error as well as the point-to-plane error, will not change given noise-less data. If noise is present, ICP will fit to the noise by detecting some local minimum, which might not correspond to the real movement. Only when movement is perpendicular to normal vectors, the estimated motion is reasonable enough[6], see Figure 4.8(c) and Figure 4.8(d). In theory, the covariance calculated in Section 4.3.2.4 should characterize such uncertainty, but in practice, the covariance is sometimes unreliable. This is also one reason why tracklets cannot be treated as tracks right from the beginning. Motion estimation for small objects in range data is sometimes unreliable, such that a pool of track hypotheses seems to be the best solution.

---

[6]The calculation of normal vectors in Section 2.4 was designed in a way to support this statement: At visible object borders, normal vectors are tilted to the back, indicating that movement can be estimated correctly within this direction.

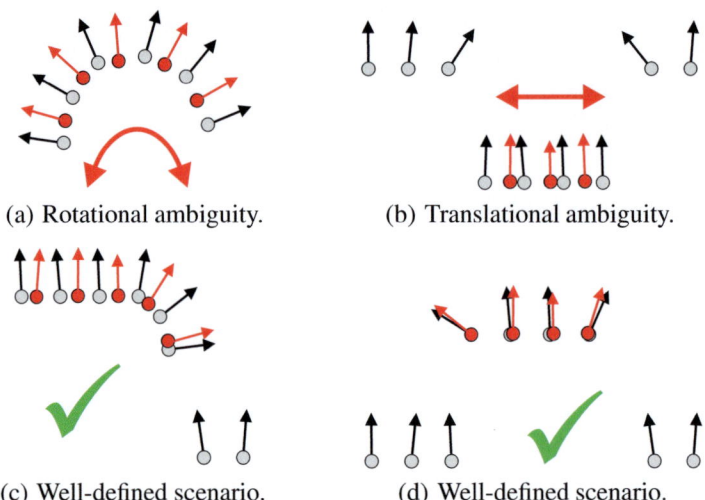

(a) Rotational ambiguity.   (b) Translational ambiguity.

(c) Well-defined scenario.   (d) Well-defined scenario.

Figure 4.8: When aligning the appearance point cloud (red) with the current scan (gray) ambiguous situations can arise: The bold red arrow indicates how the red points can be moved such that a good alignment is retained. Only the scenarios with a green checkmark have a well-defined alignment. Tilting the normal vectors at borders sideward, like the two outer red normal vectors in (d), can make a point-to-plane alignment well-defined but is effective only for objects in front of a background, see Section 2.4.

In order to characterize unreliable motion, a so-called motion histogram $m = (m_1, m_2, m_3, m_4)^\mathrm{T}$ is generated. For the tracklet that moved from $^{t-3}\rho_g$ to $^t\rho'_g$, it summarizes within four bins how many appearance points moved perpendicular to their normal vector (m_1), aslant to it (m_2 and m_3), and along the normal vector (m_4). In Figure 4.3, the red point with coordinate system is moved perpendicular to its surface direction, i.e. along its normal vector (which is not shown). The neighboring point is moved slightly aslant to its normal vector and the remaining four points strongly aslant to their normal. This would result in $m = (0, 4, 1, 1)^\mathrm{T}$.

Other characteristics are calculated for each associated track $^{t}_{*}\mathcal{T}'_h$ with association strength $a_{g,h} > 0$. As sketched in Figure 4.9, the motion of the associated track within the last 3 frames is applied to the tracklet $^{t}_{t-3}\mathcal{T}'_g$

$$^t\rho''_{g,h} = {}^{t-3}\rho_g + ({}^t\rho'_h - {}^{t-3}\rho_h) \tag{4.35}$$

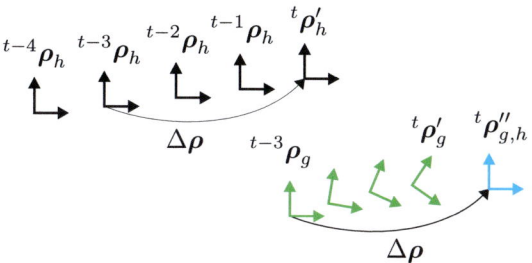

Figure 4.9: The motion $\Delta\rho$ of the last three frames of an associated track (black) is applied to the tracklet (green) resulting in a modified current pose ${}^t\rho''_{g,h}$ (blue) in place of ${}^t\rho'_g$. In case this pose fits better to the current input data, it is likely that the tracklet should be merged with the associated track.

and the ICP energy $e_g({}^t\rho''_{g,h})$ (Equation 4.13) is calculated using both the Euclidean distance d_2 (Equation 4.17) and the projective distance d_P (Equation 4.18) as d_e. These errors are denoted $e_{g,h,2}$ and $e_{g,h,P}$ in the following as opposed to $e_{g,2}$ and $e_{g,P}$, the errors for the original pose ${}^t\rho'_g$. Based on these errors the associated tracks causing minimum error can be determined as well as the track with maximum association strength

$$h_2 = \arg\min_{h:a_{g,h}>0}\{e_{g,h,2}\} \tag{4.36}$$

$$h_P = \arg\min_{h:a_{g,h}>0}\{e_{g,h,P}\} \tag{4.37}$$

$$h_a = \arg\max_{h}\{a_{g,h}\} \tag{4.38}$$

Note that h_2, h_P, and h_a are not necessarily different.

For a given tracklet ${}_{t-3}^{t}\mathfrak{T}'_g$, the feature vector $\boldsymbol{f}_g$ is created from the characteristics described above and classified with a three class support vector machine (SVM) with radial basis function (RBF) kernel [Dud01] in order to decide upon the merge of the tracklet. The optimal parameters for the SVM are derived from a manually labeled data set. This data set is also used to normalize the feature vector before classification: For each dimension independent, the training data is sorted and the upper and lower 2% quantiles are removed if at least 5 different feature values remain. The minimum and maximum value of the remaining data then define a linear scaling to the interval $[0, 1]$. This normalization is needed since SVM implementations usually assume that the different feature dimensions are in a similar range and a violation of this assumption degrades the performance of classification.

In case the SVM decided that the tracklet is to be merged, one further step remains: to decide upon which track to merge with. In this work, a score is calculated for each associated track $_*^t\mathcal{T}'_h$ with the help of a 32-dimensional feature vector $\boldsymbol{f}_{g,h}$, which includes characteristics like the association strength, tracking statistics, ICP errors when applying the motion of $_*^t\mathcal{T}'_h$, statistics of the appearance point clouds, and the motion histogram $\boldsymbol{m}$. A detailed specification of the feature values is given in Appendix A.4.2

As above, the values of the feature vector are linearly normalized to the range $[0, 1]$ using outlier-corrected sample data. A score is calculated with the help of a parameter vector $\boldsymbol{w}$ according to the linear model

$$s_h = (1 \; \boldsymbol{f}_{g,h}{}^{\mathrm{T}}) \cdot \boldsymbol{w} \tag{4.39}$$

and the associated track with the maximum score wins. The optimal values for the (1+32)-dimensional parameter vector $\boldsymbol{w}$ are determined with the help of a manually labeled data set, see Section 5.2.3.2.

4.4.3 Track Termination

Depending on the merge decision, each tracklet $_{t-3}^{t}\mathcal{T}'_g$ is either added to the set of tracks $_*^t\mathcal{T}'$, merged with an existing track, or discarded. For each track $_*^t\mathcal{T}'_h \in \, _*^t\mathcal{T}'$ it is then decided whether tracking shall be continued or terminated. In this work, tracking is terminated if either the track left the field of view, or i. e. all appearance points have a distance to the scanner above a threshold, or if the last valid measurement was made ν_{nUp} frames ago.

4.5 Mapping of Object Models

It was already discussed in Section 4.1.1 that many existing tracking methods use specific object models for specific object classes. These object models encode the appearance of an object and allow specifying the position, orientation, and size of an object by specifying parameters of the model. This makes the measurements of subsequent frames compatible and eases data association. The big disadvantage of these methods is the incapability to track objects that have not been explicitly modeled.

In this work, the model of an object is its appearance point cloud, which is constructed independently for each object on the first frame the object becomes visible. The advantage of the gained capability to track arbitrary objects is opposed to the disadvantage of having an object model, which only captures the object characteristics at that frame. When, for example, a car coming from the back passes the sensor vehicle, its appearance model mainly captures the front of that car. However, after the car has passed, its rear end is significant for accurate tracking. Hence, it is required to update the object model, i. e. the appearance point cloud, over time.

In the computer vision literature, this problem is not new. Tracking objects by their first appearance was proposed by Lucas and Kanade [Luc81] in 1981. This so-called *template tracking* has the same need for an update of the model, i. e. template. But updating the template too rapidly leads to significant drift in the estimates [Sid00]. Several possibilities to overcome drift have been published [Mat03, Jep03], but they are specialized to tracking in images. A related method for range data is the work of Gate et al. [Gat08]. They also store the appearance along with the track and update it with every new measurement. But the specific design of the approach to a 2D laser scanner prohibits its use in this work.

Akin to template-updating, but often treated as different problem, is the creation of a map in SLAM methods, see Section 1.2.1. Performing self-localization by sequential scan-matching leads to the same drift problem. A significant improvement can be accomplished by incrementally building a map. An efficient approach for dense 3D data was presented in 2011 [Moo11b]. This approach is here applied to moving objects, including the track which represents the static environment. To follow the notation of SLAM approaches, the model update is termed *moving object mapping* (MOM).

MOM is situated in the merging step, which was detailed in the previous section. There, it is described how for a tracklet $_{t-3}^{t}\mathfrak{T}_g'$ the decision is made whether to keep it, merge it with an existing track, or discard it. The former two cases are detailed in the following with the special focus on MOM.

4.5.1 Merging Tracklets

Both, the tracklet $_{t-3}^{t}\mathfrak{T}_g'$ as well as the track $_{*}^{t}\mathfrak{T}_h'$ it is merged with, are characterized by a state vector x and an appearance point cloud $\mathcal{P}^O$ which is specified relative to the object coordinate system. To ease notation, the time index t and the coordinate system reference O is omitted in the following to support readability.

In this work, a combination of the states is left out due to simplicity reasons. The state $\hat{x}_h, \Sigma_h^x$ is kept for $_{*}\mathfrak{T}_h'$, assuming that a track that exists for a longer time period is more precise than the tracklet that exists only for three frames.

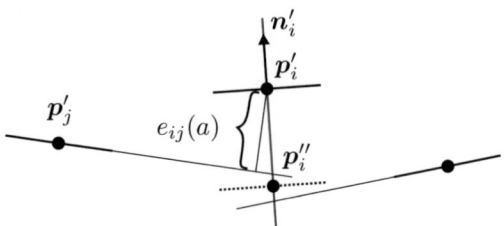

Figure 4.10: During mapping each new point p'_i is moved along its normal vector to p''_i such that it best represents a flat area together with its nearest neighbors.

In contrast, the appearance point clouds are combined. Though introduced as unordered point cloud in Section 4.3, the appearance points $\mathcal{P}$ are stored in a 3D grid with each cell containing at most one surface point. The constant grid resolution ν_{cell}, equal to the edge length of a cell, defines the level of detail of the stored object appearance. Using this grid structure, $\mathcal{P}'_g$ is integrated into $\mathcal{P}'_h$ in three steps:

First, $\mathcal{P}'_g$ is modified to $\mathcal{P}''_g$ by changing each point coordinate according to its neighbors in $\mathcal{P}'_h$. As illustrated by Figure 4.10, each point $p'_i \in \mathcal{P}'_g$ with sufficiently high flatness value is moved along its normal vector n'_i to

$$p''_i(a_i) = p'_i + a_i \cdot n'_i \tag{4.40}$$

until it best represents a plane together with the neighboring surfaces. The weighted point-to-plane energy is defined similar to the ICP energy of Equation 4.13 by

$$e_i(a) = \sum_{p_j \in \mathcal{Q}} w_{ij} \cdot \mathrm{d}_P(\mathop{\mathrm{trans}}_{O_h \leftarrow O_g} (p''_i(a)), p_j)^2$$

$$\mathcal{Q} = k \mathop{\mathrm{nn}}_{\mathcal{P}'_h} \left(\mathop{\mathrm{trans}}_{O_h \leftarrow O_g} (p'_i) \right) \tag{4.41}$$

$$w_{ij} = f_i f_j \mathop{\mathrm{rot}}_{O_h \leftarrow O_g} (n'_i)^{\mathrm{T}} n_j$$

where $k\,\mathrm{nn}$ returns the k nearest neighbors in $\mathcal{P}'_h$ and w_{ij} are weights according to the flatness values and the similarity of the normal directions. The transformation trans and rotation rot account for the different coordinate systems where the transformation is based on the poses at tracklet creation $(t-3)$. Although t would be an equally valid reference time, at $t-3$ there is no pose uncertainty in O_g since at the creation time of tracklet $_{t-3}^{t}\mathfrak{T}_g'$ the coordinate system is arbitrarily initialized and the appearance points are specified within this coordinate system, see Section 4.3. The adjustment a_i is determined by $\hat{a}_i = \arg\min_a\{e_i(a)\}$, which is a closed-form least squares solution. This adaption is the key step to account for the measurement noise of the sensor and for imprecisions in the localization and deskewing step which is detailed later on. As this adaption avoids flat areas to grow perpendicular to the plane, further localization is improved since the ICP energy function then has a well-defined minimum.

Second, each $p_i'' \in \mathcal{P}_g''$ is added to $\mathcal{P}_h'$, if the corresponding grid cell is empty. If the grid cell is occupied, its point p_j is replaced by p_i'' in case

$$\frac{r_j - r_i}{r_j} + (f_i - f_j) > \nu_{add} \tag{4.42}$$

holds. Hence, surfaces that have a higher flatness value and/or points that were captured from a lower distance replace existing surfaces in the appearance map.

Third, all points of $\mathcal{P}_h'$ are compared with the current range image. Each point is projected onto the image and its distance from the scanner is compared to the range measurement at the corresponding pixel. If a point has a shorter distance than the range measurement, the point is removed from $\mathcal{P}_h'$ since it should have been visible. For rigid objects, such a point-removal should never happen since correct tracking can only lead to occluded points. For non-rigid objects, this point-removal step is the key to successful tracking: As long as only a small portion of the appearance changes, motion can be robustly estimated by detecting outliers, see Section 4.3.2.2. Given a correct object state, the point cloud can then be updated to account for the new appearance of the object.

As described so far, the appearance point cloud is fully updated in each frame. However, this can lead to drift since motion can be described by both, a modification of the state vector, and a modification of the appearance point cloud. As consequence, the previously described combination of appearance point clouds is altered in the following way:

When a track is created, its appearance points are marked as *initial points*. When new points are added later-on, this information is used within track merging: On the one hand, an initial point is never replaced during the second step. On the other hand, the weights of an initial point in Equation 4.41 are multiplied by a factor ν_{wIP} so that the adaptation is more influenced by initial points. In a similar manner, the ICP weights in Equation 4.15 are multiplied by ν_{wIP}. In total, this significantly reduces drift but keeps mapping flexible enough to make the approach work for non-rigid objects and to allow stable tracking.

4.5.2   Keeping Tracklets

Frequently, a tracklet is kept as new track because a stationary object starts moving. In this case, the object is not only represented by the tracklet, but also by the static track since its appearance has been merged with the static track while the object was stationary. Hence, the appearance of the object has to be removed from the appearance of the static track.

More generally, keeping tracklet $_{t-3}^{t}\mathfrak{T}'_g$ makes need for postprocessing each associated track $_*^{t}\mathfrak{T}'_h$. The postprocessing is equivalent to removing the appearance of the tracklet from the appearance of the linked track. In other words, the final appearance of a track $_*^{t}\mathfrak{T}'_h$ is equal to the appearance $\mathcal{P}'_h$ before merge without the points belonging to tracklets that were kept:

$$\mathcal{P}_h = \{\boldsymbol{p}_i \in \mathcal{P}'_h : \nexists\, g, \boldsymbol{p}_j \in \mathcal{P}'_g : a_{gh} > 0 \,\wedge \mathrm{keep}(_{t-3}^{t}\mathfrak{T}'_g) \\ \wedge \left\| \boldsymbol{p}_i - \boldsymbol{p}_j \right\| < \nu_{cell} \} \tag{4.43}$$

4.6   The Static Scene

The previous pages describe in detail a fully-functioning tracking approach that includes the static scene as one track among others. Although this integrated design is an appealing concept, few separate treatments can further improve the algorithm.

4.6.1   Measurement Generation

In Section 4.3.2 it is described that an update of the state of a tracklet or track is derived by registering its appearance point cloud against the point cloud of the current scan. A big advantage of this procedure is that the measurement becomes independent from the segmentation, which results in a more stable overall approach.

For the static scene, it is more favorable to register the scan against the map, i. e. the appearance point cloud, due to three reasons: The first reason is that the (accumulated) map of the static scene is much denser than the current scan. Hence, when matching the scan against the map, the ICP will find closer, i. e. better, correspondences. The second reason is that the map potentially contains a significant area that is currently not visible. When matching the scan against the map, these areas simply remain passive, whereas the original method would have to detect these areas as outliers for whom no valid correspondences in the scan can

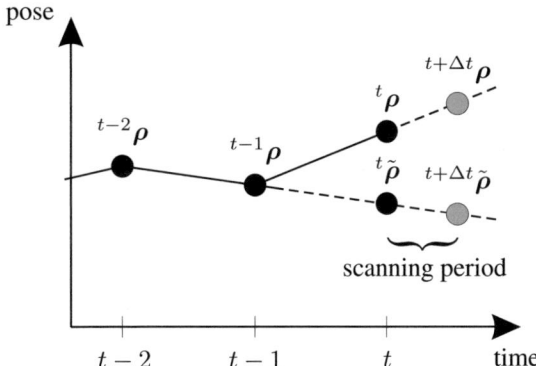

Figure 4.11: Deskewing: The pose of the vehicle with respect to the environment (black circles) can be linearly predicted (dashed lines). When capturing the data during some time period, the pose prediction is used to transform the data with respect to the predicted pose at time t. After registration, the data is once more transformed, before it is used for mapping.

be found. The third reason concerns the compensation of ego-motion: It is much easier to compensate the motion in the current scan, and accumulate the appearance within an already compensated map. Details on motion compensation are described next.

4.6.2 Deskewing

In case a sensor is used that captures a frame during some time interval $[t, t+\Delta t]$, the vehicle moves meanwhile from pose $^t\rho$ to $^{t+\Delta t}\rho$. Since at the beginning of Section 2 the assumption was made that data is represented with respect to one sensor coordinate system, the data has to be corrected according to the sensor movement. One possible solution is to estimate this movement during registration within the ICP core, as in in the work of Bosse et al. [Bos09]. However, this sophisticates the algorithm and makes need for nonlinear solvers.

Here, a much simpler but yet effective method is presented that works for all scanners which sweep the environment with a relatively high scanning rate. One example is the Velodyne scanner, shown in Figure 1.2(a), which scans the environment horizontally at a rate of ~ 10Hz.

Given the old state ^{t-1}x of the static scene track, the motion model of Equation 4.8 allows its prediction into the future. Hence, it is possible to calculate any predicted pose between $^{t}\tilde{\rho}$ and $^{t+\Delta t}\tilde{\rho}$. As sketched in Figure 4.11, these are used to transform all 3D points of the current data into the coordinate system specified by $^{t}\tilde{\rho}$. Preprocessing, feature extraction, segmentation, and registration then run on this deskewed data leading to the updated state $^{t}\boldsymbol{x}$. This state is used to deskew the original input data once more, now basing pose prediction on $^{t}\boldsymbol{x}$ instead of $^{t-1}\boldsymbol{x}$. The updated point cloud is then used for mapping, i.e. the accumulation of the appearance.

4.6.3   Map Refinement

Most SLAM methods build the map just for localization purposes. City maps, on the contrary, are mostly built using high-precision laser scanners which need several seconds or even minutes for one $360°$ scan. In the following it is shown that the accumulated map can be even further refined to obtain a final map containing more details.

The idea for refinement is similar to the adaptation step illustrated by Figure 4.10. In areas of high confidence of the normal vectors, measurements can be constricted onto a local plane. In Section 4.5.1, incoming measurements are adapted according to already existing, adapted neighbors. This is suboptimal as it first allows for increasing adaptation drift and second will not include future measurements.

To overcome these disadvantages, the map refinement builds a complete new map using the old map. In order to do so, it is here assumed that for each point $\boldsymbol{p}_i'' \in \mathcal{P}_g''$ that was added to the appearance map also the original, non-adapted measurement location $\boldsymbol{p}_i'$ is available. For each point in the existing map, k nearest neighbors are searched in a specified neighborhood and, as in Equation 4.41, the energy

$$
\begin{aligned}
e_i(a) &= \sum_{\boldsymbol{p}_j \in \mathcal{Q}} w_{ij} \cdot \mathrm{d}_P(\boldsymbol{p}_i'''(a), \boldsymbol{p}_j')^2 \\
\mathcal{Q} &= k \underset{\mathcal{P}_g}{\mathrm{nn}} (\boldsymbol{p}_i') \\
w_{ij} &= f_i f_j (\boldsymbol{n}_i')^{\mathrm{T}} \boldsymbol{n}_j'
\end{aligned}
\tag{4.44}
$$

is minimized for a in order to obtain the surface location $\boldsymbol{p}_i'''(a_i) = \boldsymbol{p}_i' + a_i \cdot \boldsymbol{n}_i'$ in the new map. Hence, the position of a point in the new map is based solely on the original positions of all points.

5 Evaluation

This chapter deals with a qualitative and quantitative evaluation of the proposed algorithms. It introduces optimizations and simplifications for the application of autonomous driving and discusses the choice of parameters for obtaining optimal results.

Evaluation is performed on sensor data captured with a *Velodyne HDL-64E S2* [Sch10], a rotating laser scanner with 64 beams that, mounted on top of a car, yields a field of view of $360° \times 28°$ with distances measured up to 120 m. With a rotation rate of 10 Hz and up to 1.3 million measurements per second the angular resolution becomes $0.18°$ horizontally and $0.44°$ vertically. The sensor is illustrated in Figure 1.2(a) and sample data is displayed in Figure 2.1 and Figure 2.2.

5.1 Preprocessing and Segmentation

The outcome of the segmentation step is the first in the processing chain that can be sufficiently evaluated. Since segmentation is closely coupled with pre-processing, these two steps are evaluated together by looking at the generated segmentation. A perfect segmentation is, however, hard to obtain. Two kinds of deviations can thereby be distinguished: *oversegmentation*, the split of the scene into too many parts, and *undersegmentation*, the merge of parts that should be separated. For the application of tracking the latter could make a moving object to remain undetected, which can possibly be fatal for autonomous driving. Thus, oversegmentation is less disadvantageous since it would only cause one object to be detected as several separate objects.

A very good overview of evaluation methods for the task of image segmentation is the work of Zhang [Zha96]. According to the author, three groups can be formed: *analytical methods*, *empirical goodness methods*, and *empirical discrepancy methods*. The first group evaluates the algorithm per se with measures like computational complexity. The second group evaluates the outcome of the algorithm, also called *machine segmentation*, by measuring inter- and intra-segment properties. The third and probably most descriptive group of methods compares the machine segmentation with a manually created reference segmentation, also called *gold standard* or *ground truth*, by calculating some error value.

Before the algorithm is evaluated in detail, some modifications are introduced in the following which optimize the approach with respect to autonomous driving.

5.1.1 Optimizations and Simplifications

The approach presented in this work is per se not limited to a specific sensor or a specific domain. However, the focus of the experimental evaluation on urban environments with one specific sensor being fixed to a car allows for some optimizations of the algorithms.

The first optimization targets on the low sensor resolution at large distances. Usually too few sensor readings derive from the same object making them not meaningful at all. Hence, measurements exceeding a certain distance ν_{rMax} are removed.

The second optimization targets on the geometry of the environment. Although the environment is fully three-dimensional, gravity allows identifying objects by their vertical structure. The latter observation is used to modify the *local convexity* criterion for segmentation: Equation 3.1 is changed into

$$c'_{i,j} = \max\left\{c_{i,j}, \min(1 - |\boldsymbol{n}_{i_z}|, 1 - |\boldsymbol{n}_{j_z}|)\right\} \tag{5.1}$$

where $c_{i,j}$ denotes the old definition and $c'_{i,j}$ the updated definition. The effect is that two points are also grouped together if both normal vectors are in a horizontal direction, i. e. if both vertical components vanish.

Note that this optimization does not, like many other works, reduce the environment to a 2D subspace. It only makes use of the direction of gravity. Objects are still detected in 3D, which allows the estimation of their motion with all six degrees of freedom.

5.1.2 Analytical Evaluation

According to [Zha96], a theoretical analysis can contain several aspects, among them being the amount of a priori knowledge, the algorithmic complexity, and the processing strategy. All three are discussed next.

One way to characterize the amount of a priori knowledge is to count the number of parameters fed into the algorithm. For the proposed approach these sum up to 17, which, if compared to other approaches, can be regarded as a relative high value. However, many publications do not detail on preprocessing which is seldom parameterless. Additionally, many parameters used in this work are physically motivated, which allows a quite good initial estimate. For further optimizing these, the reader is referred to Section 5.1.3.1 where a simple and yet effective optimization technique is presented.

The algorithmic complexity is dependent on the amount of the input data. For images this is the number of pixels n_{pix}. It is easily verified that the whole preprocessing stage is composed of local operations only. Since a fixed sequence of operations is carried out per pixel, the complexity is linear in the number of pixels: $\mathcal{O}(n_{pix})$. The same holds for the segmentation predicate, which is a local decision telling whether to connect neighboring pixels or not. The only global operation is the connected components labeling in Section 3.3. But as described in [Sha01, pp. 69–73], this can be implemented as two passes across the image. In consequence, preprocessing and segmentation work both in $\mathcal{O}(n_{pix})$. This is optimal and a big advantage over other algorithms. The relatively high portion of independent local operations thereby allows the employment of a parallel processing strategy, available e.g. on multi-core architectures or general purpose graphical processing units (GPGPUs). Hence, an implementation fulfilling real-time requirements seams feasible within the next years.

5.1.3 Empirical Evaluation

Among the empirical evaluation methods the discrepancy methods are surely the most meaningful. They compare two segmentations which both partition the set of valid pixels $\mathcal{S} = \{i\}$ into segments $\{\mathcal{S}_g \subseteq \mathcal{S}\}$, cf. Chapter 3 and Figure 5.1. The first segment set $\mathcal{M} = \{\mathcal{S}_g \subseteq \mathcal{S}\}$ is the machine segmentation, which is the outcome of the algorithm to be evaluated. The second segment set $\mathcal{G} = \{\mathcal{S}_g \subseteq \mathcal{S}\}$ is the ground-truth segmentation, which represents the optimal segmentation. The ability to calculate an objective error can be used to compare different algorithms and to optimize parameters.

Several error functions have been proposed [Hoo96, Car05, Dou11], each proposal having in mind a specific target application. As stated above, oversegmentation is less severe than undersegmentation. Such an asymmetric error e_p was introduced by Cardoso et al. [Car05]. Given two segmentations $\mathcal{A}$ and $\mathcal{B}$, the error $e_p(\mathcal{A}, \mathcal{B})$ is equivalent to the minimum number of pixels that must be deleted from $\mathcal{S}$ (and consequently from $\mathcal{A}$ and $\mathcal{B}$) so that segmentation $\mathcal{B}$ is a refinement of segmentation $\mathcal{A}$. For details on how to calculate this error see Appendix A.5.

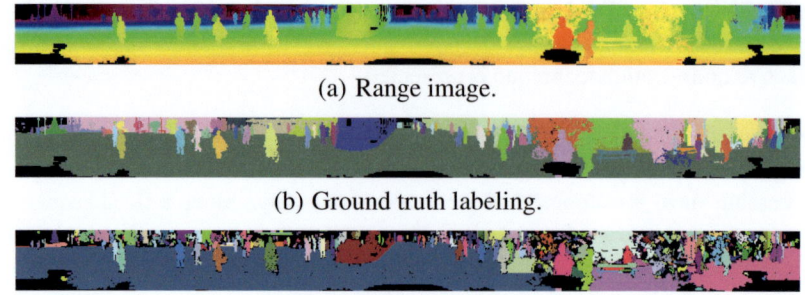

(a) Range image.

(b) Ground truth labeling.

(c) Segmentation result.

Figure 5.1: Segmentation result compared against ground truth. Each segment is displayed in a different color.

Based on this asymmetric pixel error, two errors are defined: e_o which penalizes oversegmentation and e_u which penalizes undersegmentation:

$$e_o = e_p(\mathcal{M}, \mathcal{G}) \tag{5.2}$$
$$e_u = e_p(\mathcal{G}, \mathcal{M}) \tag{5.3}$$

Both errors are zero if the two segmentations are identical. e_o increases if oversegmentation is present, e_u increases as soon as segments exist within $\mathcal{M}$ that cross borders of the ground truth segmentation. Thus $e_o + e_u = 0$ holds *iff* $\mathcal{G} = \mathcal{M}$.

A third error is defined which characterizes missing pixels: As stated in Section 3.3, the implemented algorithm might reject pixels due to bad neighboring connections. This number of valid pixels not contained in any resulting segment constitutes the third error:

$$e_m = \sum_{i \in \mathcal{S}} (1 - \mathbf{1}_{\mathcal{M}}(i)) \tag{5.4}$$

The indicator function $\mathbf{1}$ returns 1 if the element is in the specified set and 0 otherwise.

The total segmentation error e_s used within this work is a linear combination of the three errors defined above:

$$e_s = c_o \cdot e_o + c_u \cdot e_u + c_m \cdot e_m \tag{5.5}$$

The constants are chosen so that undersegmentation is the most severe nuisance followed by missing pixels and oversegmentation: $c_o = 2$, $c_u = 30$, $c_m = 3$.

5.1.3.1 Parameter Selection

As already discussed, reasonably good initial parameters are not hard to determine since most parameters are physically motivated. However, an optimization is desirable. Using the above defined error function, this goal fits into the general optimization scheme. There, an error can be calculated for any given parameter vector and the goal is to find the parameter vector which minimizes the error. Many optimization techniques exist for various types of problems. Evolutionary algorithms [Whi01] lend themselves for the given problem since they can handle both discrete and continuous values as well as non-continuous error functions. Using the implementation of Keijzer et al. [Kei02] and four hand-labeled ground truth segmentations, the following parameter values were finally selected:

Table 5.1: Selected parameter values

parameter	value	description	page
ν_{rMax}	80 m	maximum range value	66
ν_{hPix}	5 pix	maximum interpolation, horizontally	15
ν_{vPix}	2 pix	maximum interpolation, vertically	15
ν_{iMax}	0.5 m	maximum interpolation interval	15
ν_{sMax}	0.2 m	maximum smoothing interval	15
ν_{rDiff}	0.148	soft threshold on range value change	16
ν_{rNDiff}	1.90782	soft threshold on neighbor-relative change in range values	16
$\nu_{rNF}(r)$	$2 \cdot \exp(-0.14 \cdot r) + 0.25$	tangent slope at ν_{rNDiff}	16
ν_{rSB}	0.03 m	range difference to detect shadow border	18
ν_{wOB}	2	object border weight for border measure	18
ν_{fDec}	0.5	decay factor for flatness measure	19
ν_{nSim}	14.8062°	normal similarity soft threshold	26
ν_{nSimF}	10	tangent slope at ν_{nSim}	26
ν_{conv}	-7.67°	convexity soft threshold	26
ν_{convF}	1.165	tangent slope at ν_{conv}	26
ν_{st}	0.45	segmentation decision threshold	27
ν_{minPix}	8 pix	minimum segment size	30

5.1.3.2   Results

Using the same optimization procedure as for parameter selection, the proposed approach is compared against the original local convexity criterion [Moo09]. The error after optimization serves as goodness measure for comparison. Three methods are compared: The original criterion with both, parameter values fixed to the published values and parameter values optimized, the proposed method from Chapter 3, and the proposed method with adjustments for vehicular environments (Section 5.1.1). Further comparison against other methods is desirable but not easily possible because the implementations of the respective authors are not available and because a standardized comparison process is not yet established in the scientific community. Hence, a quantitative evaluation of the proposed segmentation is limited to the results listed in Table 5.2.

Table 5.2: Comparison of segmentation methods

Method	Over-segmented Pixels e_o	Under-segmented Pixels e_u	Missing Pixels e_m	Weighted Error e_s
Original criterion [Moo09], parameters as specified	55.2%	0.77%	11.0%	4.22%
Original criterion [Moo09], parameters optimized	26.5%	0.88%	9.36%	2.73%
Generic method (Chapter 3)	29.9%	0.46%	12.9%	2.85%
Extended method (Section 5.1.1)	26.6%	0.58%	11.8%	**2.69%**

The listed values are based on four hand-labeled ground truth segmentations, one is shown in Figure 5.1(b). The values e_o, e_u and e_m are normalized by the summed pixel count $n_{pix} = 55680$, the weighted summed error e_s is normalized by $n_{pix} \cdot (c_o + c_u + c_m)$, cf. Equation 5.5. The high portion of oversegmented pixels derives from the ground truth labeling: it is chosen to identify the different objects although different parts of an object are not necessarily connected in the image. Hence, the segmentation method will split such objects apart. Since both the floor and the background typically cover a large part of the image, a high portion of the pixels are counted as oversegmented pixels, though the results can be considered to be very good. This behavior becomes apparent at the bottom right

(a) Side street: Buildings and parked cars at the left and right, a van up front.

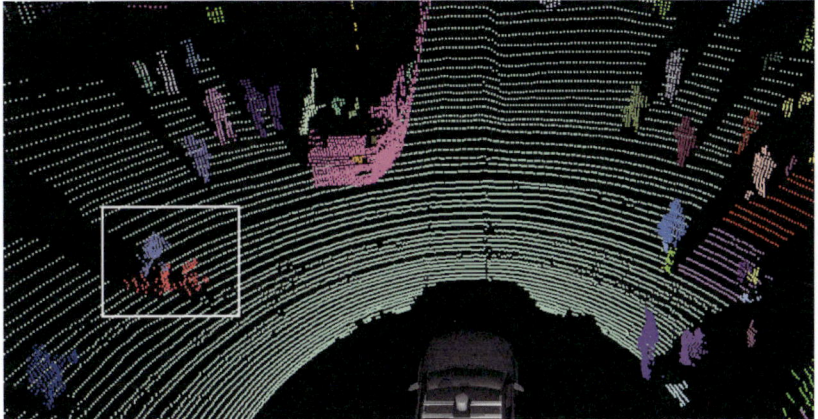

(b) Pedestrian zone: A cyclist (rectangle) detected as two separate objects, a tram (pink), and many pedestrians.

Figure 5.2: Segmentation results, different colors represent different segments.

of Figure 5.1(c), where the floor is separated into three objects. Furthermore, the used range data contains systematic errors in the close range. This leads to further divisions of the ground plane, see Figure 5.3 and Figure 5.4, and hence to even more pixels being counted as oversegmentation.

On examining the total error in Table 5.2, it can be recognized that the proposed extended method achieves the lowest error among the evaluated meth-

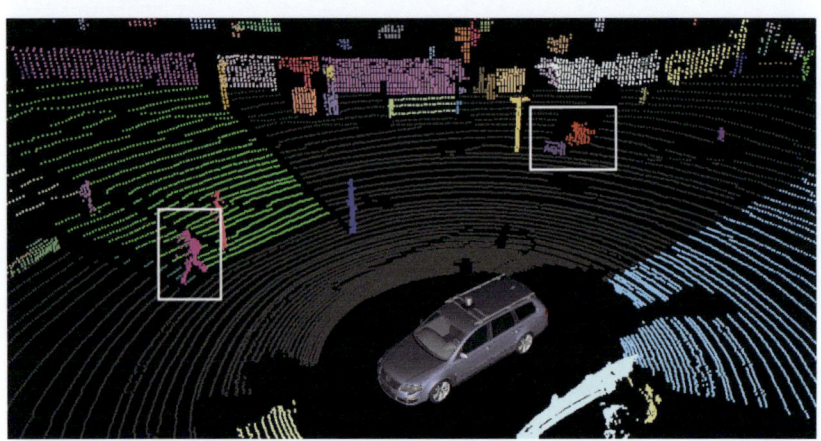

(a) A pedestrian (left rectangle) and a recumbent bicycle with trailer (right rectangle) crossing an intersection.

(b) Highway scenario with many cars and bushes on the lower right corner.

Figure 5.3: Continued segmentation results as in Figure 5.2.

(a) Tram stop: Pedestrians next to a delivery van.

(b) Tunnel with four trucks on the opposing lanes (from left to right in pink, green, the rectangle, light-green). Segmentation splits apart the semitrailer truck (rectangle), which is beneficial for tracking (the trailer has a rotational degree of freedom with respect to the tractor).

Figure 5.4: Continued segmentation results as in Figure 5.2.

ods followed by the parameter optimized original criterion, the proposed generic method, and the unoptimized original criterion. The results for the original criterion reveal that though a manual choice of parameters can yield good results, an optimization can significantly improve performance. From further discussions the unoptimized original criterion is excluded.

Important seems to be the specialization term of Equation 5.1 since the two best methods contain this criterion (though in a slight variation). Advantageous is also the formulation of the segmentation criteria in a fuzzy-logical manner combined with the introduction of *extended convexity*, which is the main difference between the original criterion and the proposed extended method. The effect is in particular a significant decrease of the number of undersegmented pixels, which is beneficial for object detection and tracking, as discussed at the beginning of Section 5.1.

Further evaluation of the proposed segmentation method concentrates on qualitative results. In Figure 5.2, Figure 5.3, and Figure 5.4, the segmentation outcome is shown for several different environmental settings. Common to all results is a high capability of the method to detect arbitrary objects ranging from pedestrians over cyclists, cars, and trucks up to trams. Even very rare objects like recumbent bicycles with trailer are successfully detected, see Figure 5.3(a). This capability of the proposed method to be robust to unexpected data is an important prerequisite for autonomous systems. The probably greatest weakness concerns vegetation, see Figure 5.3(b): Small leafs make a reliable estimation of the object geometry impossible, which is the basis of the proposed method. As a result, bushes and trees decompose into many small segments, prohibiting a reliable estimation of motion. However, the impact of this weakness to autonomous driving is small: Since bushes and trees do not move, reliable motion estimation is not required.

5.2   Motion Estimation

The most complex part of the proposed work is motion estimation. It results in an estimate of the pose of the sensor with respect to the starting point and in a set of objects that are detected to move. In the following, the different parts of the proposed algorithm are evaluated in detail.

5.2.1 Optimizations and Simplifications

Like in the previous section, further optimization of the algorithms with respect to autonomous driving is possible. These optimizations are described next; a detailed evaluation is given afterwards.

5.2.1.1 Speed-Up

The bottleneck of the motion estimation method is the registration procedure described in Section 4.3.2, which aligns a tracklet g with the current scan. Most time is spent on finding the nearest neighbors for the $n_{pt} = |\mathcal{P}_g|$ appearance points in each iteration. One possibility to reduce the effort is to use only a subset of the appearance points, as discussed in [Rus01]. Especially for large tracklets, subsampling speeds up the algorithm without degrading accuracy, which is not the case for small tracklets. Hence, the number of selected surfaces n_{sel} is a sublinear function on the number of original surfaces n_{pt}:

$$n_{sel} = \nu_{nMin} + \sqrt{\max\{0, n_{pt} - \nu_{nMin}\}} \tag{5.6}$$

with ν_{nMin} being a constant specifying the minimum number of points to use. Very important for the accuracy is the method of subsampling, see [Gel03]. Here, one half of the target points is sampled uniformly according to the 3D location; the other half is sampled uniformly according to the direction of the normal vector. This guarantees to retain diversity in both, object structure and local shape.

As described in Section 4.6.1, registering the static scene in a special way can improve robustness: Instead of aligning the static scene track with the current scan, the scan is aligned with the map of the static scene. Hence, subsampling has to take place for the scan, not for the track. Here, $n_{up} = \nu_{nStUp}$ points are sampled uniformly from the upper half of the range image and $n_{lo} = \nu_{nStLo}$ points are sampled uniformly from the lower half image area. For the specific case of the Velodyne laser scanner, sampling more points from the upper image results in more points on buildings since the lower half of typical range images contains the ground and closely moving objects. To avoid sampling points from moving objects, the registration results of all other tracks are used: Each track appearance is projected onto the image and the corresponding pixels are unmasked. Hence, moving objects are explicitly taken into account, in contrast to many other SLAM methods, see Section 4.1.2.

An alternative way to speed-up the registration procedure is presented in [Qiu09]. Moving nearest neighbor search to a graphical processing unit allows executing the search in parallel, which accelerates computation massively. But since the cost of implementation is high, this alternative was not used within this work.

5.2.1.2   Small Objects

An optimization targeting at the robustness of the approach concerns the handling of small objects during registration. Small objects give rise to only a few point correspondences. These do not allow estimating the six degrees of freedom robustly. Hence, for objects with $|\mathcal{P}| < \nu_{nRed}$ the degrees of freedom are reduced to four by assuming the pitch and roll angles to be constant. For the application area of this approach such a reduction holds for nearly all kind of movements. Possible violations to this assumption can be compensated by dynamic mapping.

5.2.1.3   Neighbor Search

One further optimization is application specific. In German city-like environments vehicles move with up to 50 km/h. Relative to the sensor, vehicles on the opposite lane enter the field of view with up to 100 km/h. At this speed, objects translate by 2.8 m between frames at a sensor frequency of 10 Hz. On rural roads this number can increase up to 5.6 meters. Such a high initial transformation is a huge challenge for the ICP algorithm, which is designed to search only locally. As a solution, Douillard et al. [Dou12] propose segment matching to get the initial transformation, but the method seems to work not robustly enough for arbitrary types of scenarios. Another solution is feature matching [Moo10]. But because movements occur mainly in the horizontal xy plane, even simpler and faster is to modify the correspondence search. Stretching the vertical coordinates by a factor of ν_{zFac} in the nearest neighbor search, retrieves horizontally displaced points in favor of vertically displaced points. By applying this stretching in the very first registration step of a new tracklet only, the update of longer existing track(let)s is not altered. Experiments show the success of this small modification.

5.2.2   Analytical Evaluation

Consistent with the analysis in Section 5.1.2, the following aspects are discussed next: The amount of a priori knowledge, the algorithmic complexity, and the processing strategy.

The number of explicit parameters of the proposed motion estimation approach is comparable to other methods. However, the proposed approach is very generic,

i. e. it works in 3D for any kind of object class. Hence, no special motion and appearance model is used. This is opposed to many other methods, which employ specific models that can be regarded as additional a priori knowledge. Hence, the proposed motion estimation method can be seen as a method using comparably little a priori knowledge.

The algorithmic complexity of motion estimation can be analyzed according to Figure 4.1, where estimation proceeds in several steps. The first step at time t is marked *Prediction*. For each track(let) independently, the Kalman Filter (KF) is used to predict the current state, leading to a complexity linear in the number of track(let)s $n_{trk} = n_{t1} + n_{t2} + n_{t3} + n_{t*}$ with $n_{t1} = \left| {}_{t-1}^{t-1}\mathcal{T} \right|$ etc. In the *Registration* step, track(let)s get aligned with the current scan by means of the ICP algorithm. As discussed in Section 4.3.2, a k-d tree is built in advance for the current scan to speed-up neighbor search, an operation that is in $\mathcal{O}(n_{pix} \cdot \log n_{pix})$. When using the special treatment of the static scene according to Section 4.6.1, another k-d tree is built on the appearance of the static track with size n_0. Each track(let) $\mathcal{T}_g$ is subsampled according to Equation 5.6, an operation linear in the size of the appearance $n_{app} = |\mathcal{P}_g|$. The subsampled points are aligned during several iterations n_{it} by searching for each point the closest neighbor in the k-d tree. Hence, the registration of one track(let) is in $\mathcal{O}(n_{app} + n_{it} \cdot \sqrt{n_{app}} \cdot \log n_{pix})$ and for the static scene track in $\mathcal{O}(n_{pix} + n_{it} \cdot (n_{up} + n_{lo}) \cdot \log n_0)$. Updating the KF with the registration result is constant for each track(let). The next step is entitled *Merging*. For each tracklet in ${}_{t-3}^{t}\mathcal{T}'$ independently, all n_{ass} associations are processed where errors are calculated on the appearance using the k-d tree. Decisions are then made in constant time, since both the classifier and the linear score model are only dependent on the feature dimensionality. Unless the decision was to ignore the tracklet, the appearance points are adapted and inserted into the merged track and the corresponding points in all associated tracks are removed. Since the appearance is stored within a grid structure, access is in constant time, leading to the complexity $\mathcal{O}(n_{t3} \cdot n_{ass} \cdot n_{app} \cdot \log n_{pix})$ for *Merging*. At last, new tracklets are created from the object hypotheses and associations are established to existing track(let)s. Since their projections were already computed in the registration step, one simple pass across the image is enough. Altogether, motion estimation is in

$$
\begin{aligned}
\mathcal{O}(n_{trk} &+ n_{pix} \log n_{pix} + n_0 \log n_0 \\
&+ \left(n_{app} + n_{it} \cdot \sqrt{n_{app}} \cdot \log n_{pix} \right) \cdot n_{trk} \\
&+ \left(n_{pix} + n_{it} \cdot (n_{up} + n_{lo}) \cdot \log n_0 \right) \\
&+ n_{trk} \\
&+ n_{t3} \cdot n_{ass} \cdot n_{app} \cdot \log n_{pix} \\
&+ n_{pix})
\end{aligned}
\tag{5.7}
$$

With n_{it} being a constant small number, n_{t3} being a fraction of and thus being upper-bound by n_{trk}, and $(n_{up} + n_{lo})$ usually being in the order of $\sqrt{n_{pix}}$, the above can be simplified to

$$
\begin{aligned}
\mathcal{O}(n_{pix} & \log n_{pix} \\
& + n_0 \log n_0 \\
& + \sqrt{n_{pix}} \cdot \log n_0 \\
& + n_{trk} \cdot n_{ass} \cdot n_{app} \cdot \log n_{pix})
\end{aligned}
\tag{5.8}
$$

In the worst case, the number of associations n_{ass} might grow up to the number of tracks n_{t*}, which is also a fraction of n_{trk}, making the approach quadratic in n_{trk}. Since the object hypotheses generation step is preferred to oversegment and hence is preferred to create many track(let)s, this leads to a complex algorithm. But in practice, n_{ass} is constantly small, allowing removing it from Equation 5.8. Of the remaining variables, only n_{trk}, n_{app}, and n_0 change over time. n_{trk} is high if many moving objects exist and if many object hypotheses are created, which is the case in environments with many small objects. n_{app} and n_0 both increase over time, since appearance is accumulated. However, both converge since the level of detail of the appearance point clouds is fixed and points are removed if they move out of the viewing range. All in all, the algorithm can be rated to be modestly complex, mainly because the dependence on the input data is only loglinear and the dependence on the number of tracks is only linear. However, the sizes of the appearance point clouds have a significant impact on the complexity and techniques for efficiently managing and reducing them can be a key to speed-up the algorithm.

One possible speed-up was presented by Qui et al. [Qiu09]. They move nearest neighbor search to a graphical processing unit, which allows the execution of the search in parallel. Although the effort for implementation was beyond the scope of this work, its application to the presented approach is possible. Additionally, multi-core CPUs can be exploited since a parallel processing strategy is prevalent in the whole approach: Prediction, registration, update, and merging are to most parts independent for each track(let). As a consequence, a real-time implementation should be feasible.

5.2.3 Empirical Evaluation

Although motion estimation jointly localizes the sensor vehicle with respect to the environment and detects and tracks moving objects, joint evaluation is difficult. One reason is that localization is performed even if no moving objects exist. It can even be performed independently from moving object tracking since a special static scene track is created from the very first frame. As detailed in Section 4.6, it even allows for special optimizations. Another reason is that localization is based on a much higher portion of the sensor data and thus has a potentially higher quality. Hence, the following evaluates the localization capabilities first based on recorded sequences that do not contain moving objects. The detection and tracking of moving objects is evaluated thereafter in two sections, one evaluating the merging step, one the tracking quality. For all experiments, the parameters are fixed to the values listed in Table 5.3.

Table 5.3: Selected parameter values for tracking

parameter	value	description	page
ν_{ptpl}	0.7	avg. flatness value to use point-to-plane ICP	46
ν_{dMax}	16.6 m	distance normalization for ICP weight	47
ν_{wMin}	1	minimum accumulated ICP weight	48
ν_{itMin}	4	minimum number if ICP iterations	48
ν_{itMax}	10	maximum number if ICP iterations	48
ν_Δ	0.01	maximum relative distance change	48
ν_{dz}	2	maximum Mahalanobis distance from predicted measurement	49
ν_{nUp}	30	maximum number of measurement failures	58
ν_{cell}	0.1 m	grid resolution	60
ν_{add}	0.3	threshold to replace appearance points	61
ν_{wIP}	2	ICP weight for initial points	61
ν_{nMin}	500	minimum number of sampled appearance points	75
ν_{nRed}	10k	number of appearance points to switch between 6/4DOF estimation	76
ν_{zFac}	5	stretch of vertical coordinates at first neighbor-search	76
ν_{nStUp}	3000 pix	points sampled from upper image	75
ν_{nStLo}	1000 pix	points sampled from lower image	75

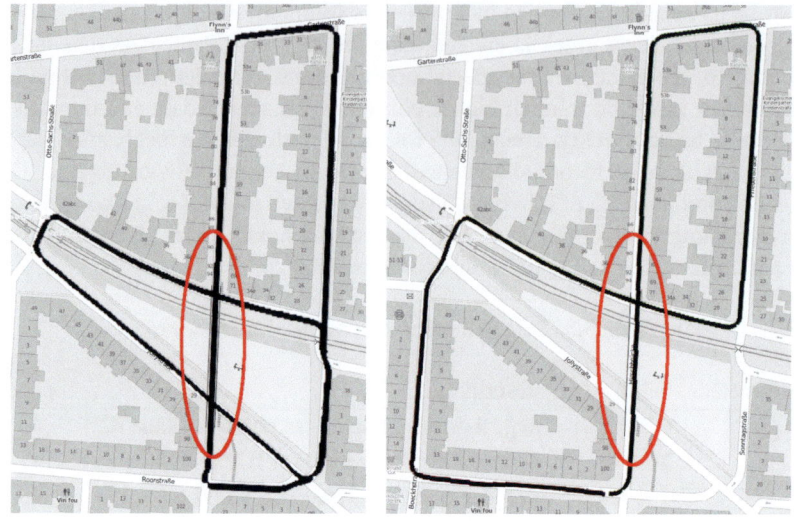

(a) Scenario 1, length = 1.3 km.   (b) Scenario 2, length = 1.1 km.

Figure 5.5: Bird eye's view of the scenarios used for localization evaluation. The black curves are the result from the proposed method. In both scenarios the vertical crossing in the middle, marked by a red ellipse, is a bridge across two streets. Background images are courtesy of OpenStreetMap.

5.2.3.1   Localization

For each incoming frame, the proposed algorithm always outputs the position and orientation of the sensor with respect to the starting position. The estimate is based upon matching the current input data with the accumulated map, which makes the localization estimate being influenced by two sources of error: First, sensor data noise leads to an absolute positioning error within the current map at each frame. Second, errors are introduced into the map since the map extension is based upon the estimated (noisy) pose leading to a steadily increasing drift.

In order to evaluate the absolute positioning error, a highly precise map and alternative sensors capable to determine the correct pose are required. Both are difficult to obtain. Hence, evaluation here concentrates on the second source, which also dominates the first source as soon as the sensor is significantly moved.

In order to evaluate drift, precise pose estimates are necessary, too. These are possible to obtain for scenarios containing loops: As soon as the sensor car returns to the position where it started, the precise pose can be determined by matching the

Table 5.4: Influence of the algorithm stages on the end point error.

Setting	Mapping	Deskewing	Adaptation	Error
Scenario 1				
1	no	no	no	19.60 m
2	no	no	yes	19.33 m
3	no	yes	no	27.41 m
4	no	yes	yes	27.21 m
5	yes	no	no	4.47 m
6	yes	no	yes	4.13 m
7	yes	yes	no	2.90 m
8	yes	yes	yes	2.29 m
INS	–	–	–	3.30 m
Scenario 2				
1	no	no	no	22.25 m
2	no	no	yes	22.09 m
3	no	yes	no	18.58 m
4	no	yes	yes	18.89 m
5	yes	no	no	8.08 m
6	yes	no	yes	7.36 m
7	yes	yes	no	4.81 m
8	yes	yes	yes	4.10 m
INS	–	–	–	2.64 m

sensor data against the initial map, e. g. by means of the ICP algorithm. Though the first error affects this reference pose, it can be neglected if the drift error rose up to a significant level.

Two scenarios were recorded with the experimental vehicle *AnnieWay* [Moo11b] in the city of Karlsruhe and are depicted in Figure 5.5. Both do not contain any moving object and allow evaluating the localization performance independent from the detection and tracking of moving objects.

In order to evaluate drift, it must be guaranteed that the algorithm cannot make use of the loop-closure. This property is assured by discarding parts of the map as soon as they get out of the viewing range of the sensor, which is limited to 50 m for this experiment. Hence, the initial map is not present any more when the car returns to the starting point. The Euclidean distance between the estimated end position and the reference end position constitute the errors listed in Table 5.4.

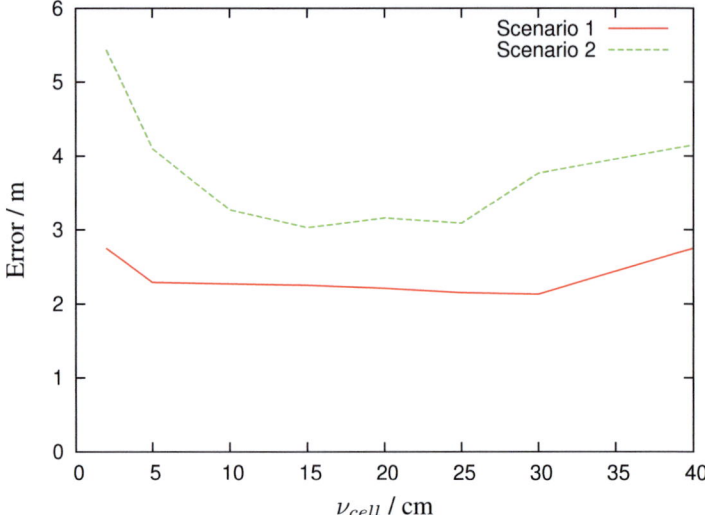

Figure 5.6: Influence of the grid resolution ν_{cell}, i.e. the level of detail used for appearance mapping, on the localization drift. The error measures the deviation between the estimated end position and the true end position.

The influence of the different stages of the algorithm that affect localization performance is evaluated by (de)activating various combinations. Setting 5 thereby corresponds to approaches doing incremental scan-matching [Nü07] and setting 7 is comparable to the work of Bosse et al. [Bos09]. As expected, using pairwise scan-matching only (i.e. setting 1-4) results in very high errors, whereas with activated mapping localization is much more precise. According to Figure 5.6, the grid resolution ν_{cell} can thereby be chosen in a wide range – only the detail of the map suffers for high values of ν_{cell}. Not accounting for the sensor rotation is the second principal influence of localization error. The linear interpolation used in this work thereby shows its effectiveness. Finally, adapting measurements while adding them to the map again improves the results.

Interesting is also a comparison of the estimated trajectory with the recordings of an integrated navigation system (INS) which fuses GPS, wheel speed sensors and inertial measurements. Local errors of the INS are much higher than those of the proposed method. This is typical for the evaluated scenarios, since in street canyons only few satellites are visible and GPS signals are sometimes reflected leading to wrong estimates. Even after driving more than one kilometer, the

Figure 5.7: Generated map for scenario 1 from a perspective view. Color encodes altitude from green (low) over blue and red up to yellow (high).

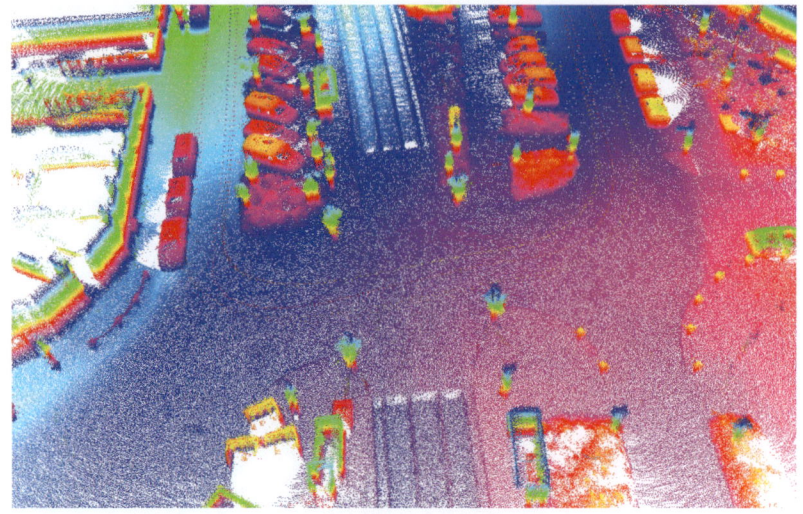

(a) Railroad crossing.

(b) Bridge crossing a street with staircases.

Figure 5.8: Enlarged parts of the map of scenario 1. Color encodes altitude.

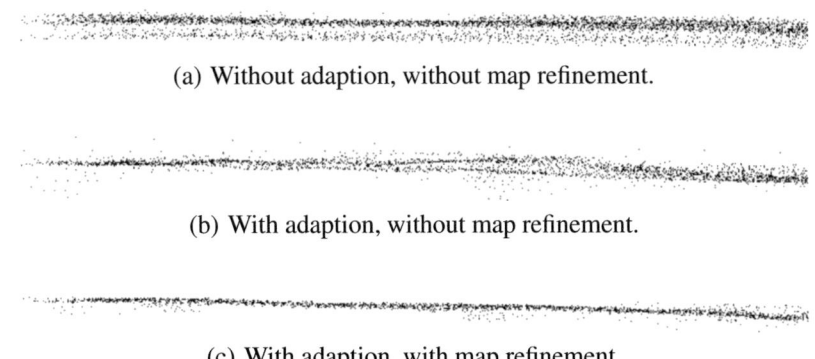

(a) Without adaption, without map refinement.

(b) With adaption, without map refinement.

(c) With adaption, with map refinement.

Figure 5.9: Side view of a local point cloud of a road surface from the accumulated map shown in Figure 5.8 for three different algorithm settings.

accumulated error of the proposed method is in the same range as the error of the INS.

Another focus of the evaluation is the quality of the produced map. The more detailed the map is, the better it can be used for other purposes, as e. g. city modeling. As this is hard to evaluate quantitatively, the accumulated maps are here examined visually. A sample map is shown in Figure 5.7, two enlarged parts are shown in Figure 5.8. The map exhibits detailed object contours especially for buildings, parked cars, and the street surface. The latter is shown in a side-view in Figure 5.9 for three algorithm variants. It is clearly visible that both, adaptation during mapping as well as the map refinement step, help in getting detailed surfaces. This not only makes the city model more appealing, it also improves localization since new data can then be aligned uniquely with the map.

The results show that the algorithm can be used for both, precise localization and city model building. The grid size ν_{cell} is thereby the main parameter to choose. A low value allows for highly precise maps, a higher value for faster (on-line) processing.

5.2.3.2 Merge Decisions

As soon as moving objects are present, these must be identified in the merging stage, see Section 4.4.2. In this stage, it is decided for each tracklet $_{t-3}^{t}\tilde{\Sigma}'_{g}$ whether to keep it as track, whether to merge it with an existing track, or whether

Table 5.5: Classification results on a labeled data set for two different parameter settings of the classifier. These parameters allow balancing the misclassifications among the classes.

		Decision variant A			Decision variant B		
		Keep	Merge	Ignore	Keep	Merge	Ignore
Class	Keep	23	14	89	103	13	10
	Merge	0	12208	612	196	12516	108
	Ignore	1	208	3614	200	567	3056
	Accuracy		94.49%			93.48%	

to ignore it. Therefore, a feature vector f_g describing the tracklet is classified by a support vector machine (SVM) with radial basis function (RBF) kernel [Dud01] with radius $\gamma = 0.01$. Obviously, a good performance of the classifier is a key aspect to a robust tracking approach.

In order to train and evaluate the classifier, a labeled data set was set-up containing 16769 feature vectors in total. The data set is representable for urban traffic with 126 tracklets being kept, 12820 being merged, and 3823 being ignored. The unequal class distribution poses a challenge to the classifier and comes from the fact that most parts of the environment are static and that once a moving object is detected, the subsequent hypotheses are merged into the existing track. Though the full dataset was used to train the classifier for subsequent experiments, evaluation was carried out by executing 4-fold cross-validation[1].

Classification statistics are given in Table 5.5 for two different parameter settings of the classifier. In variant A, a high penalty is set on wrong detections (decision = keep) leading to a classifier that classifies only a small percentage (23/126) of the "keep" examples correctly but classifies only one of the other examples as "keep". As a consequence, the set of tracks consists with a high certainty of tracks that are really moving. In variant B, a high penalty is set on missed detections. Hence, most of the moving objects (103/126) are immediately detected, but even more other objects (196+200) are erroneously detected as well leading to a low precision.

Many more variants exist that balance the different misclassifications in various ways. By fusing the classes "Merge" and "Ignore" into only one class, a binary

---

[1]The dataset is split into 4 disjoint subsets with equal class distribution. In each of four rounds, training is performed on the union of three of the subsets and evaluation is carried out on the remaining subset. Results from the four rounds are gathered to constitute the final evaluation result.

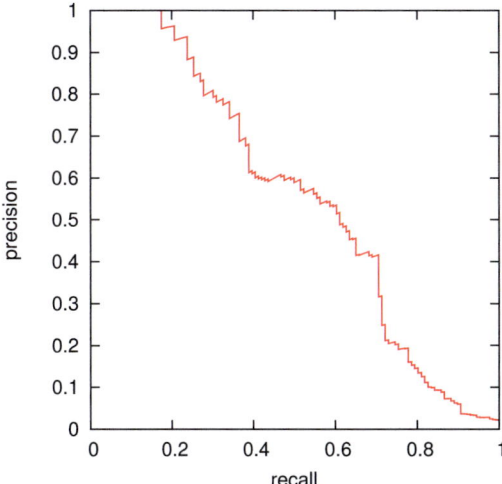

Figure 5.10: Performance of the trained classifier. When tuning it for merge decisions, a trade-off between precision (ratio of detections that are correct) and recall (ratio of objects that are detected) has to be made. The higher both are, the better the classifier is. The final choice depends on the application.

classification problem is obtained that allows the characterization of the balancing with only one parameter. By varying this parameter, different classifiers are obtained that can be characterized by their precision and recall ratio, see Figure 5.10.

Although the precision-recall curve is close to the diagonal and not close to the upper right corner, the classification accuracy reaches nearly 95% at some points of the curve. This can be regarded as very good. Misdetections occur mainly on slowly moving objects. These are difficult to detect since they move only by centimeters within the verification interval of three frames. But since misdetections are on a frame-wise basis, objects might nevertheless be detected (and correctly tracked) in subsequent frames.

In case a tracklet $_{t-3}^{t}\mathfrak{T}_g'$ is to be merged, a target track must be selected from the set of associated tracks. According to Section 4.4.2, a score $s_h = \left(1\ \boldsymbol{f}_{g,h}^{\mathrm{T}}\right) \cdot \boldsymbol{w}$ is calculated for each association h characterized by a feature vector $\boldsymbol{f}_{g,h}$ and the maximum score determines the target track. Finding the optimal parameter vector $\boldsymbol{w}$ is non-trivial; it is especially not possible to cast this problem into an efficient optimization framework since the number of associations varies. In this work, w is determined in two steps using a labeled data set containing 3917 feature vectors representing 1471 tracklets with 2.66 associations in average.

In the first step, each association i. e. feature vector is considered independently. The set of feature vectors is split into two classes, one containing the correct associations, the other containing the wrong associations. A linear SVM with class labels 1 and -1 is then used to find the optimal hyperplane w_{init}. Although the *maximum score per tracklet* rule was not considered correctly, a robust maximum margin estimate is attained.

In the second step, w_{init} is refined to yield optimal assignment accuracy. Evolutionary algorithms [Whi01] are applied to find the optimized w_{opt} using a score equal to the sum of wrong target tracks multiplied by $0.001 \cdot \|w_{opt} - w_{init}\|$, the deviation from the initial robust estimate. For the given training data, a decision accuracy of 96.94% is reached, which can be regarded as high.

5.2.3.3 Tracking Quality

In order to evaluate the tracking quality, a special experiment was conducted using a second car, termed *target car*, with built-in precise sensors for position, speed, and acceleration. The beginning of the experiment is depicted in Figure 5.11(a) where the target car starts immediately in front of the sensor car. Both cars accelerate differently and their distance increases up to 32 m, see Figure 5.12(a). The sensor car then approaches and overtakes the target car at $t = 24,6$ s. The true speed of the target car, determined with the help of an integrated navigation system and ranging from 0 up to 60 km/h, is compared against the speed estimated by the proposed tracking method. Since the estimates of the proposed method are relative to the sensor, the speed of the car was determined as the norm of the vectorial difference between the velocity of the car and the velocity of the static scene.

The proposed tracking method with moving object mapping (MOM) is compared against two variations with modified mapping strategy: one using the fixed appearance point cloud from the first detection, the other replacing the appearance point cloud each frame with new measurements. The run of the speed-error curves are shown in Figure 5.12(b) and detailed characteristics are given in Table 5.6. Note that for a wide range of target distances the magnitude of the speed error stays in a similar range.

Replacing the appearance each frame leads to the worst result. As argued in Section 4.5, this technique leads to a strong drift which is expressed by high speed errors. The fast changing appearance also causes tracks to get lost easily

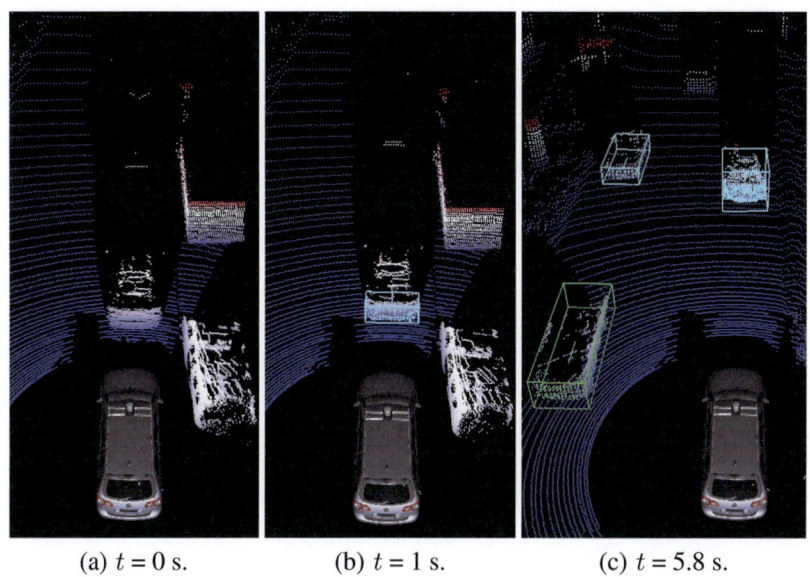

(a) $t = 0$ s.   (b) $t = 1$ s.   (c) $t = 5.8$ s.

Figure 5.11: Tracking result: Each detected object is marked by a cuboid in a unique color. The car in front of the sensor car is the special target car used for assessing the tracking quality. It is detected as moving 1s after acceleration started and continuously tracked together with other moving objects like e. g. cars on the opposing lane.

Table 5.6: Tracking statistics for speed comparison experiment of Figure 5.12 generated without outer 10% quantiles.

	number of tracks	speed error median	speed error mean	speed error std-deviation
with MOM	2	-0.84 m/s	-0.96 m/s	±1.16 m/s
first appearance	4	-0.82 m/s	-1.04 m/s	±1.29 m/s
replace appearance	12	-10.62 m/s	-7.69 m/s	±10.27 m/s

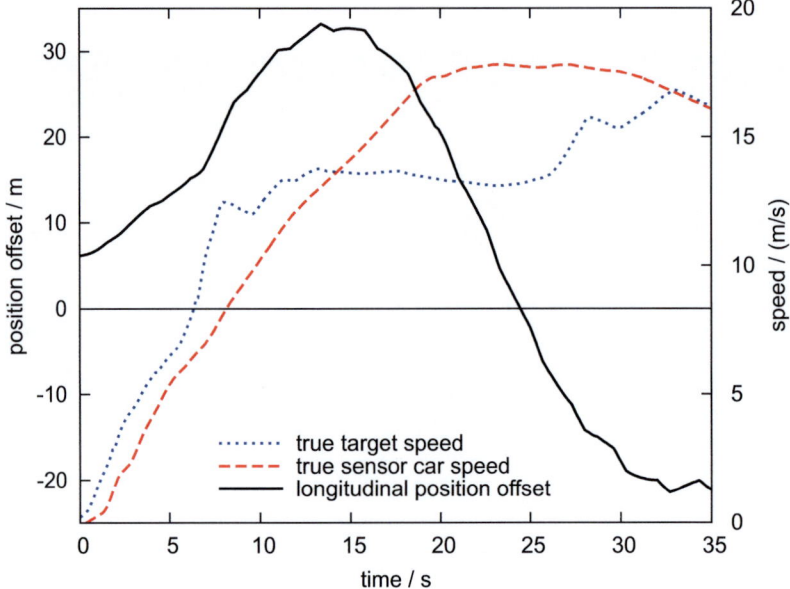

(a) Speed profiles of both cars and longitudinal position of the target car with respect to the sensor car.

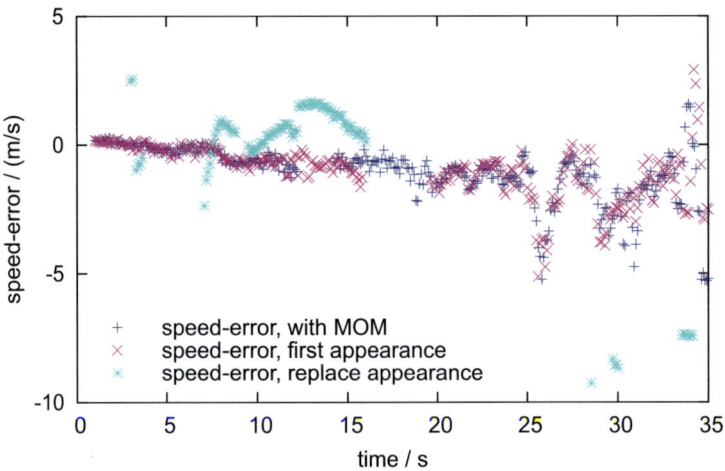

(b) Comparison of the estimated speed with the true target speed for different tracking strategies. Missing values indicate temporary tracking failures.

Figure 5.12: Tracking quality, assessed by using a target car with precise sensors.

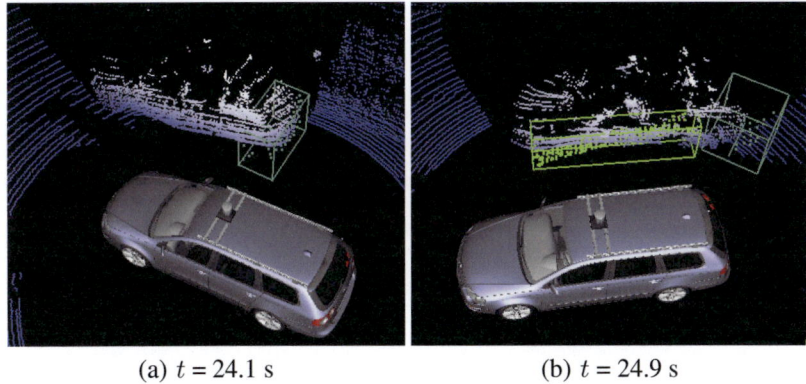

(a) $t = 24.1$ s   (b) $t = 24.9$ s

Figure 5.13: Tracking without Moving Object Mapping: When passing by a vehicle, the appearance cannot adapt to the changed viewpoint and a new track is instantiated.

if track-associations are inadequate. This disadvantage is expressed by the high number of tracks corresponding to the second vehicle.

The other two variants exhibit only few differences since the viewpoint onto the target car changes only once. Hence, the first appearance characterizes the target as favorable as the mapped appearance for a large part of the sequence. The difference becomes noticeable in the time range 25-30 s of the sequence when the sensor car passes by the target car. If only the first appearance is used, the track is lost since the appearance only characterizes the back of the car, see Figure 5.13. As consequence, a new track is created that represents the side of the car, which is again replaced later on by a track that represents the front of the car. With activated MOM, the appearance smoothly adapts to the viewpoint changes and tracking is successfully continued during the whole overtaking maneuver, as depicted in Figure 5.14. This ability to adapt is also expressed in Table 5.6 by the lower number of associated tracks. However, the relatively high speed error during overtaking cannot be prevented by MOM since the estimation of motion parallel to surface planes is very unreliable in range data.

Additional experiments were conducted in environments containing many moving objects. Figure 5.15, Figure 5.16, Figure 5.17, and Figure 5.18 show results of a long sequence recorded at an intersection in the city of Karlsruhe. In the beginning, the sensor vehicle stands still and immediately detects and tracks moving objects like cars and pedestrians, see Figure 5.15(b). Only two slowly

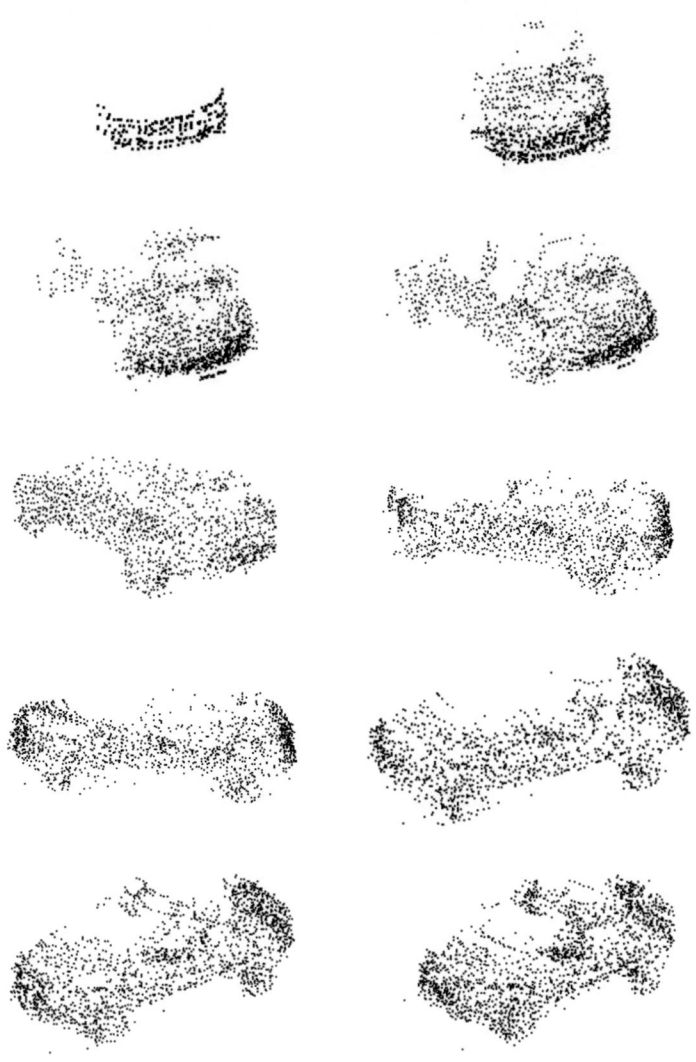

Figure 5.14: Moving Object Mapping: Appearance of a car accumulated over time (from left to right, from top to bottom). Initial points are depicted with double size (well visible in the upper four images).

(a) Beginning of sequence, $t = 0$ s.

(b) After verification interval, $t = 0.4$ s.

Figure 5.15: Tracking result: Nearly all moving objects are immediately detected and tracked. Each tracked object is displayed by a cuboid and the appearance points in a unique color. The cuboid, or bounding box, is calculated in a postprocessing step from the appearance.

(a) $t = 7$ s. MOM helps bridging occluded areas, e.g. for the turquois car.

(b) $t = 14.3$ s. The current approach does not reason about overlapping areas.

(c) $t = 18.4$ s. As soon as the cars in front start moving, they are detected.

Figure 5.16: Tracking result continued from Figure 5.15.

(a) Current sensor data, the sensor car is right of the image.

(b) Tracks displayed by bounding box and appearance points.

Figure 5.17: Tracking result continued from Figure 5.15 at $t = 26.6$ s. The result of MOM is clearly visible on the truck and the following four cars when comparing the tracks to the (sparse) sensor data.

Figure 5.18: Tracking result continued from Figure 5.15 at $t = 28$ s. Objects ranging from pedestrians over cyclists, cars and vans are successfully tracked across the whole intersection.

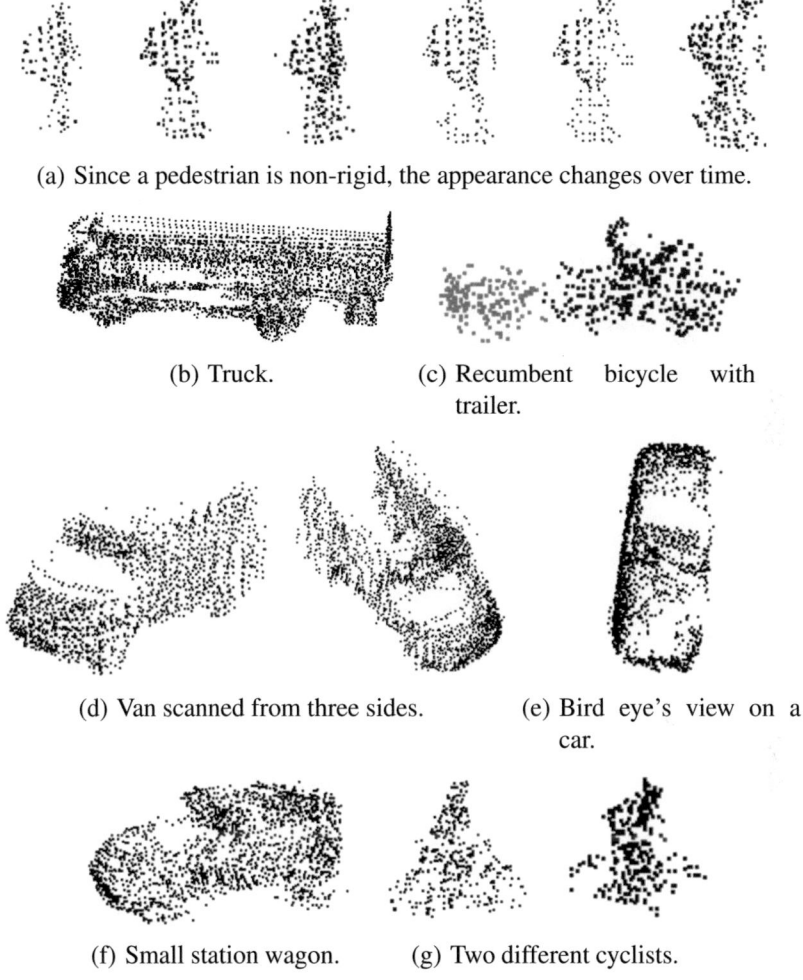

(a) Since a pedestrian is non-rigid, the appearance changes over time.

(b) Truck.

(c) Recumbent bicycle with trailer.

(d) Van scanned from three sides.

(e) Bird eye's view on a car.

(f) Small station wagon.

(g) Two different cyclists.

Figure 5.19: Moving Object Mapping: More appearance point clouds accumulated over time.

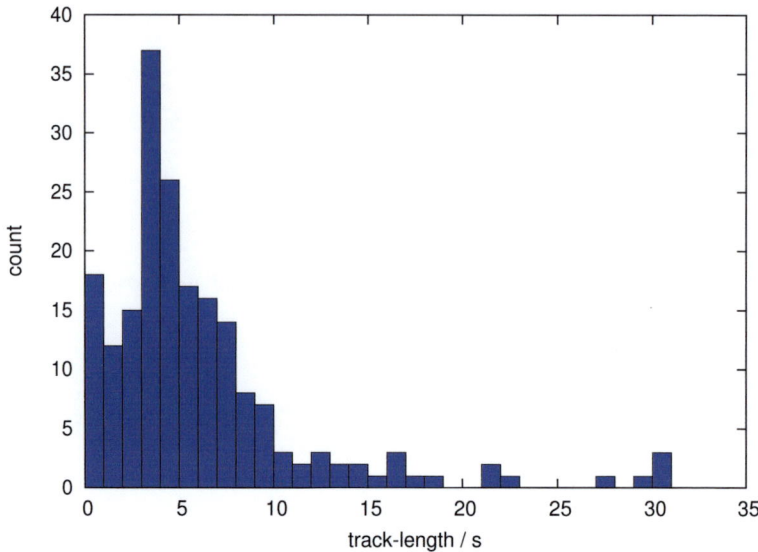

Figure 5.20: Track lengths on the sequence illustrated in Figure 5.15 (total 50 s).

moving pedestrians (close to the right image border) are not detected and tracked immediately but 0.3 s later (not shown).

As illustrated in Figure 5.16(a) and Figure 5.16(b), MOM helps to keep the identity of objects even if the object is partly occluded. However, the proposed method does not reason about overlapping areas. Hence, the appearance of two tracks can occupy the same volume, as illustrated in Figure 5.16(b). Thus, merging overlapping tracks could constitute a possible extension of the proposed method. The preserved object details due to MOM are especially visible in Figure 5.17 when comparing the sparse sensor data with the accumulated object appearance and also in Figure 5.20, which shows the accumulated object appearance for several diverse objects.

After approximately 18 s, the traffic light turns green and the sensor car starts crossing the intersection together with the cars on the same and neighboring lane. As illustrated once more in Figure 5.16(c), the proposed approach is able to immediately detect the object movements. Figure 5.18 shows the tracking output after the sensor car finished crossing the intersection. Most moving objects are correctly detected and tracked. Only a few cars on the opposing lanes are not detected owing to the occlusions caused by stationary (waiting) cars on the closest opposing lane (left of the sensor vehicle). For the tracked objects, the detailed accumulated appearances indicate that the objects were successfully tracked over a long time period, since the object outlines of three sides are visible. This claim is confirmed by Figure 5.20 that shows the distribution of the track lengths for this intersection experiment. The few close-by cars are tracked successfully from the time they start moving (at around 20 s) until the end of the sequence (at 50 s). Most other objects are tracked for a significant period of time, too.

One further observation can be made in Figure 5.18: The approach is not only able to track objects in the close vicinity but also at farer distances. Especially objects moving in the same direction as the sensor car are even tracked at far distances when being only partially visible.

All in all, the proposed method is able to detect and track moving objects of various types, in various distances and at various speeds. Object identities are seldom lost and kept even when objects are partly occluded. This property is especially advantageous for extended perception systems that focus on object relations.

6 Conclusion and Outlook

One of the biggest challenges to turn autonomous cars into reality is to develop a reliable on-board perception system. This work built upon recent developments in sensor technology and introduced innovative ideas for two major perception tasks: the self-localization of an autonomous car and the detection and tracking of moving objects. One major advantage of this work is the joint treatment of both problems which particularly improves the self-localization capabilities.

Input to the proposed method is a sequence of dense 3D measurements obtained by a range sensor. The advantages of such sensors are manifold: Most important is that the environment is captured in a sufficiently dense resolution in order to detect any relevant object. The precise range measurements allow the estimation of the speed of other traffic participants even at far distances. Since they implicitly measure free space they also allow designing a simple fallback level for safe operation at low speeds if other algorithms fail.

The presented work proposed a complete processing chain which starts with efficient preprocessing and feature extraction. Already at this point, object borders are detected by a unique method which is based on the difference of distance measurements. Its explicit integration into the estimation of local surface planes stands out against other methods. By additionally assessing the appropriateness of the estimated surface planes, profound knowledge about the surface geometry of the environment is available for further processing.

A key component of the presented work is a generic method for the detection of objects. The observation that objects as diverse as trees, cars, or humans are all largely composed of convex parts led to an original criterion. Convexity is evaluated locally and adjacent measurements are grouped if they are convex but not separated by an object border. This efficient detection method splits apart the set of range measurements, with each fraction representing a hypothesized object. The main advantage of the local convexity criterion is its ability to detect arbitrary objects in nearly any situation.

Another key component of the presented work is a joint method for object tracking and localization. Each hypothesized object is tracked over time by aligning its initial distance measurements with the current measurements. Thus, the position and velocity of objects can be estimated independently from new object hypotheses, making the estimation very robust. By treating the static scene as one object, the position and orientation of the sensor car is estimated with respect to the static scene, which corresponds exactly to the localization task. The association of tracked object hypotheses with existing tracks and the decision whether a hypothesis represents a new object is carried out by a novel track management system. By casting the problem as classification task, the possibility to resort to intensively studied methods was enabled.

Since the relative viewpoint onto moving objects changes, the alignment of the initial measurements of a track with the current measurements can fail after some time. Moving object mapping solves this problem. For each object the measurements are integrated over time in order to combine the appearance from different viewpoints. Since the static scene is also treated as an object, the proposed approach implicitly builds a map of the environment which can be seen as a 3D city model. This city model can be further refined by a technique proposed in this work: In flat areas the 3D point measurements are contracted to yield sharper surface edges.

The proposed approach was evaluated on collected sensor data from inner-city scenarios using a 64-beam laser scanner. The approach was shown to yield excellent localization estimates. Drift is by an order of magnitude lower than common methods using cameras. The object detection and tracking was shown to work very reliably with various object classes including cars, cyclists, pedestrians, trucks, and trams.

Despite the successful application of the proposed algorithms on experimental data, further developments are possible. One potential extension concerns the object detection method: The integration of multiscale features can lead to a better compensation of sensor noise and will result in superior detection results.

Future line of work can also focus on the improvement of the tracking performance. By merging neighboring tracks that move in parallel, bigger tracks can be formed which lead in general to more robust tracking results. By postponing uncertain merge-decisions, a better detection rate may be achieved. By including appearance features (e. g. from cameras), the correspondence search can be supported with the effects of getting more robust velocity estimation and increasing the maximum detection speed. Implementing specific motion models for specific object classes will make state estimation more robust. Even further, the use of a street-map allows bridging larger observation gaps since the motion prediction will be more accurate. Modeling interactions between objects can also lead to improved tracking results.

One last line of future research can focus on achieving a real-time implementation. Some possibilities were already discussed in this work, namely the usage of general-purpose graphical processing units, multi-core CPUs, and the *single instruction multiple data* features of modern CPUs. These are all applicable to the proposed approach owing to the parallel design of the proposed algorithms. Another significant speed-up can be obtained by classifying object hypotheses in order to early reject static objects like trees or buildings. As a consequence, the computational load can be significantly reduced.

Despite the focus of the experiments to vehicular environments, the design of the proposed approach allows its use in other areas as well. The generic design for three-dimensional environments and the tracking with six degrees of freedom even permit its use for flying robots. Continuing the line of research into these areas will be fascinating.

A Appendix

A.1 Coordinate Systems and Transformations

The present work uses right-handed, orthonormal coordinate systems C. A given C_1 can be transformed into an arbitrary C_2 by a translation and rotation.

In 3D, the translation can be parameterized by the vector $\boldsymbol{t} = (t_x, t_y, t_z)^\mathrm{T}$. Hence, when translating C_1 by $\boldsymbol{t}$ to yield C_2, a point $\boldsymbol{p}_1$ in C_1 will become

$$\boldsymbol{p}_2 = \boldsymbol{p}_1 - \boldsymbol{t} \tag{A.1}$$

in C_2.

A rotation can be represented in various ways, including rotation angles, one rotation vector, one rotation matrix, or quaternions. In this work, rotation angles and rotation matrices were used. Exemplary, a rotation by an angle ψ around the coordinate axis z is expressed by the rotation matrix

$$\boldsymbol{R_z} = \begin{pmatrix} \cos\psi & \sin\psi & 0 \\ -\sin\psi & \cos\psi & 0 \\ 0 & 0 & 1 \end{pmatrix}$$

where the rotation angle is specified in a counter-clockwise direction when viewing the rotation axis from the top. Then, a point $\boldsymbol{p}_1$ specified in the original C_1 can be expressed in the new C_2 by

$$\boldsymbol{p}_2 = \boldsymbol{R_z} \cdot \boldsymbol{p}_1 \tag{A.2}$$

Similarly, a rotation by an angle θ around the coordinate axis y and a rotation by the angle ϕ around the coordinate axis x are expressed by

$$\boldsymbol{R_y} = \begin{pmatrix} \cos\theta & 0 & -\sin\theta \\ 0 & 1 & 0 \\ \sin\theta & 0 & \cos\theta \end{pmatrix}, \boldsymbol{R_x} = \begin{pmatrix} 1 & 0 & 0 \\ 0 & \cos\phi & \sin\phi \\ 0 & -\sin\phi & \cos\phi \end{pmatrix}$$

When rotating C_1 in the order ψ (around z), θ (around y), ϕ (around x) to obtain C_2, the rotation matrices can be combined into

$$\boldsymbol{R_{xyz}} = \boldsymbol{R_x} \cdot \boldsymbol{R_y} \cdot \boldsymbol{R_z} \tag{A.3}$$

which is one possibility to implement the rotation operator $\underset{C_2 \leftarrow C_1}{\text{rot}} (\cdot)$.

The combination of translation and rotation is coded by the 6D pose vector $\rho = (\phi, \theta, \psi, x, y, z)^T$. Its implementation yields the transformation

$$p_2 = \underset{C_2 \leftarrow C_1}{\text{trans}} (p_1) = R_{xyz} \cdot (p_1 - t) \tag{A.4}$$

The inverse transformation can be derived using linear algebra:

$$p_1 = \underset{C_1 \leftarrow C_2}{\text{trans}} (p_2) = R_{xyz}^{-1} \cdot p_2 + t \tag{A.5}$$

where the inverse of a rotation matrix is equal to its transposed:

$$R^{-1} = R^T \tag{A.6}$$

A.2   The Kalman Filter

This section summarizes the equations needed to implement the state filtering described in Section 4.3. For the derivation of the equations and other details, the reader is referred to the works of Bar-Shalom et al. [BS87, BS02].

The goal of the Kalman Filter (KF) is to estimate an uncertain state x at discrete time steps $t, t+1, t+2, \ldots$, where the state at time t is represented by a normal distribution with mean $^t\hat{x}$ and covariance $^t\Sigma^x$. On each time step t, two actions are carried out: prediction and update.

In the prediction step, the last estimate $^{t-1}\hat{x}, ^{t-1}\Sigma^x$ of the state is predicted to the current time using the linearized motion model of Equation 4.10. Hence, the predicted estimate $^t\tilde{x}, ^t\tilde{\Sigma}^x$ is

$$^t\tilde{\hat{x}} = M_{xx} \cdot {}^{t-1}\hat{x} \tag{A.7}$$
$$^t\tilde{\Sigma}^x = M_{xx} \cdot {}^{t-1}\Sigma^x \cdot M_{xx}^T + {}^{t-1}\Sigma^v \tag{A.8}$$

assuming zero-mean noise $\hat{v}$. The expected measurement can be calculated using the measurement model of Equation 4.9

$$^t\tilde{\hat{z}} = M_{zx} \cdot {}^t\tilde{\hat{x}} \tag{A.9}$$
$$^t\tilde{\Sigma}^z = M_{zx} \cdot {}^t\tilde{\Sigma}^x \cdot M_{zx}^T + {}^t\Sigma^w \tag{A.10}$$

assuming zero-mean noise $\hat{w}$. The difference between the expected measurement and the real measurement ${}^t\hat{z}$ yields the innovation

$$
{}^t i = {}^t\hat{z} - {}^t\hat{\hat{z}} \tag{A.11}
$$

and the filter gain

$$
{}^t G = {}^t\tilde{\Sigma}^x \cdot M_{zx}^{\mathrm{T}} \cdot ({}^t\tilde{\Sigma}^z)^{-1} \tag{A.12}
$$

The state is finally updated giving rise to the new estimate

$$
{}^t\hat{x} = {}^t\hat{\bar{x}} + {}^t G \cdot {}^t i \tag{A.13}
$$
$$
{}^t\Sigma^x = (I - {}^t G \cdot M_{zx}) \cdot {}^t\tilde{\Sigma}^x = {}^t\tilde{\Sigma}^x - {}^t G \cdot {}^t\tilde{\Sigma}^z \cdot {}^t G^{\mathrm{T}} \tag{A.14}
$$

It can be seen that the uncertainty of the state always increases in the prediction step and decreases in the update step, though the increase and decrease may be infinitely small.

The initialization of the state vector is discussed in Section 4.3 and the measurement generation in Section 4.3.2.4 includes the estimation of noise ${}^t\Sigma^w$. Missing is a discussion about an appropriate choice for the initial state covariance ${}^0\Sigma^x$ and the motion model noise ${}^t\Sigma^v$.

The motion model noise ${}^t\Sigma^v$ characterizes the inaccuracy of the motion model. In this work, it is assumed that objects move with constant velocity which is definitely violated at traffic lights. Thinking about a maximum acceleration a_{max} of objects leads to a maximum error in position ($0.5 \cdot a_{max} \cdot \Delta t^2$) and velocity ($a_{max} \cdot \Delta t$) of the state. These values then compose ${}^t\Sigma^v$ on the diagonal with the off-diagonals being zero assuming that all components of the state vector are independent.

Similarly, the initial state covariance ${}^0\Sigma^x$ can be designed. Assuming a maximum velocity of objects[1] directly leads to the entries on the lower half diagonal. The upper half diagonal characterizes the position uncertainty which can be set equal to the measurement uncertainty of the sensor. Again, off-diagonals are set to zero assuming that all components of the state vector are independent

---

[1]The maximum velocity must be given with respect to the sensor. Assuming that cars drive with up to 50 km/h in inner cities, the relative speed might reach 100 km/h.

A.3 Estimating the Transformation between Point Clouds

The estimation of the transformation between two point clouds is at the very heart of the ICP algorithm [Che91, Bes92] used in Section 4.3.2. Given a set of weighted point correspondences $\{(w_i, \boldsymbol{p}_i, \boldsymbol{q}_i)\}$, the function

$$e(\boldsymbol{\rho}) = \sum_i w_i \cdot \mathrm{d}_e(\mathrm{trans}_{\boldsymbol{\rho}}(\boldsymbol{p}_i), \boldsymbol{q}_i)^2 \qquad (A.15)$$

defines an error over the correspondences. This error is equal to the error in Equation 4.15 if $\boldsymbol{q}_i$ corresponds to the nearest neighbor of $\boldsymbol{p}_i$ in $\mathcal{P}^S$ determined by using the last transformation $\boldsymbol{\rho}_{k-1}$. Several error or energy functions are possible for d_e, see Section 4.3.2. In this work both the Euclidean distance d_2 and the projective distance d_P are used. The final goal is to find a transformation that minimizes the overall-error:

$$\boldsymbol{\rho}_k = \arg\min_{\boldsymbol{\rho}}\{e(\boldsymbol{\rho})\} \qquad (A.16)$$

where the pose $\boldsymbol{\rho}_k$ can also be represented by a rotation matrix $\boldsymbol{R}_k$ and a translation vector $\boldsymbol{t}_k$ as described in Appendix A.1.

A.3.1 Euclidean Point-to-Point Error

When using the Euclidean distance d_2 as d_e, like Besl et al. [Bes92], a closed-form solution to Equation A.16 exists. The estimation of the rotation decouples from the estimation of the translation. With

$$\overline{\boldsymbol{p}} = \frac{\sum_i w_i \boldsymbol{p}_i}{\sum_i w_i}, \quad \overline{\boldsymbol{q}} = \frac{\sum_i w_i \boldsymbol{q}_i}{\sum_i w_i} \qquad (A.17)$$

being the weighted centroids of the two point clouds, a covariance matrix can be calculated by

$$\boldsymbol{C} = \sum_i (\boldsymbol{q}_i - \overline{\boldsymbol{q}}) \cdot w_i \cdot (\boldsymbol{p}_i - \overline{\boldsymbol{p}})^{\mathrm{T}} = \boldsymbol{U}\boldsymbol{S}\boldsymbol{V}^{\mathrm{T}} \qquad (A.18)$$

that can be factored using singular value decomposition. The rotation matrix is then determined by

$$\boldsymbol{R}_k = \boldsymbol{U}\boldsymbol{V}^{\mathrm{T}} \qquad (A.19)$$

In case the determinant $|R_k|$ is smaller than zero, R_k is re-calculated by

$$R'_k = U \cdot \mathrm{diag}(1, 1, |R_k|) \cdot V^{\mathrm{T}} \tag{A.20}$$

The translation vector is finally determined by

$$t_k = \overline{q} - R_k \cdot \overline{p} \tag{A.21}$$

For a detailed derivation of this solution see the work of Horn et al. [Hor87].

A.3.2 Projective Point-to-Plane Error

When using d_P as d_e, like Chen et al. [Che91], the correspondence set must be extended by the normal vectors n_i at q_i yielding the correspondence set $\{(w_i, p_i, q_i, n_i)\}$. The error function can then be rewritten using a rotation matrix and a translation vector:

$$e(\rho) = \sum_i w_i \cdot \left[(R_\rho \cdot p_i + t_\rho - q_i)^{\mathrm{T}} n_i \right]^2 \tag{A.22}$$

To the best of my knowledge, no complete derivation of a solution to the minimization of this equation was yet published. Hence, the complete derivation is included in this work for the sake of completeness.

The minimization of Equation A.22 is not straight-forward, since R is an orthonormal matrix with only three free parameters. But since the rotation angles are usually small, first-order Taylor-expansion can be applied leading to the linearized rotation matrix

$$R_\rho \approx \begin{pmatrix} 1 & -\psi & \theta \\ \psi & 1 & -\phi \\ -\theta & \phi & 1 \end{pmatrix} \tag{A.23}$$

Combining A.23 and A.22 and rearranging with $t_\rho = (t_x, t_y, t_z)^{\mathrm{T}}$ yields

$$
\begin{aligned}
e(\rho) &= \sum w_i [(p_{i,x} - \psi p_{i,y} + \theta p_{i,z} + t_x - q_{i,x}) n_{i,x} + \\
&\qquad (\psi p_{i,x} + p_{i,y} - \phi p_{i,z} + t_y - q_{i,y}) n_{i,y} + \\
&\qquad (-\theta p_{i,x} + \phi p_{i,y} + p_{i,z} + t_z - q_{i,z}) n_{i,z}]^2 \\
&= \sum w_i [(p_i - q_i)^{\mathrm{T}} n_i + t^{\mathrm{T}} n_i + \phi(p_{i,y} n_{i,z} - p_{i,z} n_{i,y}) + \\
&\qquad \theta(p_{i,z} n_{i,x} - p_{i,x} n_{i,z}) + \psi(p_{i,x} n_{i,y} - p_{i,y} n_{i,x})]^2 \\
&= \sum w_i [(p_i - q_i)^{\mathrm{T}} n_i + (c_i^{\mathrm{T}}, n_i^{\mathrm{T}}) \rho]^2
\end{aligned}
$$

where $c_i := p_i \times n_i$ denotes the cross product between point and normal. The above formulation can be transformed into matrix form with

$$
A := \begin{pmatrix} c_1^{\mathrm{T}} & n_1^{\mathrm{T}} \\ c_2^{\mathrm{T}} & n_2^{\mathrm{T}} \\ \vdots & \vdots \\ c_2^{\mathrm{T}} & n_n^{\mathrm{T}} \end{pmatrix}, \; b := \begin{pmatrix} -(p_1 - q_1)^{\mathrm{T}} n_1 \\ -(p_2 - q_2)^{\mathrm{T}} n_2 \\ \vdots \\ -(p_n - q_n)^{\mathrm{T}} n_n \end{pmatrix}, \; W := \begin{pmatrix} w_1 & & 0 \\ & \ddots & \\ 0 & & w_n \end{pmatrix}
$$

leading to:

$$
\begin{aligned}
e(\rho) &= (A\rho - b)^{\mathrm{T}} W (A\rho - b) \\
&= \rho^{\mathrm{T}} A^{\mathrm{T}} W A \rho - 2\rho^{\mathrm{T}} A^{\mathrm{T}} W b + b^{\mathrm{T}} W b
\end{aligned}
$$

Since this term is quadratic in ρ, there exists exactly one value for ρ that minimizes the error $e(\rho)$. By setting the derivation to zero, the estimation is obtained as:

$$
\hat{\rho} = (A^{\mathrm{T}} W A)^{-1} A^{\mathrm{T}} W b \tag{A.24}
$$

Since the above estimation corresponds to the least squares estimation it is bias-free in case the observations b are bias-free [Sti06].

In case $A^{\mathrm{T}} W A$ is not a full-rank matrix it is not invertible. This can be the case if e. g. the transformation between two (infinite) planes is to be estimated, where only the translation in normal vector direction and two rotations can be determined. One solution is to bias the estimate towards zero by inverting a regularized matrix $(A^{\mathrm{T}} W A + \sigma_r^2 \cdot I)^{-1}$ instead. The coefficient σ_r^2 should be chosen at least one order of magnitude smaller than the measurement noise. In the current implementation it was set to $\sigma_r^2 = 10^{-6}$. Obviously, the resulting estimate is not anymore bias-free.

In any case, the estimation is based on a linearized error function. Hence, the estimated rotations are only reasonable if they are small enough. In order to prevent invalid large rotations, the estimated rotations are limited to $[-5°, 5°]$ in the implementation. Note that this limitation only applies to the estimated transformation in each ICP iteration. The total transformation can nevertheless be estimated for larger rotations.

A.4 Feature Vectors for Track Management

Given a tracklet $_{t-3}^{t} \mathcal{T}_g'$ and some linked tracks $_{*}^{t} \mathcal{T}_h'$ with association strength $a_{g,h} > 0$, feature vectors are calculated to decide about track merging, see Section 4.4.2. These feature vectors are composed of characteristics which are detailed in the following. For values that do not exhibit a balanced distribution, a logarithmic scaling is applied according to

$$\log_{sp}(x) = \log(1 + \max\{0, x\}) \tag{A.25}$$

A.4.1 Classification

For the tracklet g with the associated tracks h_2, h_P, and h_a, the 52-dimensional feature vector $\boldsymbol{f}_g$ is composed of

[1] $\in \{0, 1\}$ is 1 if the last measurement was successful and 0 otherwise.

[2] $\in \{0, 1, 2, 3\}$ is equal to the number of measurement failures.

[3] $= \log_{sp} \left\| ({}^t\boldsymbol{x}'_g - {}^{t-1}\boldsymbol{x}_g) - ({}^{t-1}\boldsymbol{x}_g - {}^{t-2}\boldsymbol{x}_g) \right\|$ characterizes if the two last relative movements were approximately the same.

[4] $= e_{g,P}$ characterizes the point-to-plane error at the last measurement.

[5] $= e_{g,2}$ characterizes the point-to-point error at the last measurement.

[6] $\in \{0, 1, 2, 3\}$ characterizes when the last successful measurement was made.

[7] $= \log_{sp}(|\mathcal{P}_g|)$ characterizes the size of the appearance point cloud.

[8] characterizes for the bin of the motion-histogram with the highest value the average move in meters within the last three frames in direction of the normal vector.

[9] $= \log_{sp}(m_4)$ characterizes the number of normal vectors being parallel to the direction of motion.

[10] $= \log_{sp}(m_3)$ characterizes the number of normal vectors being slightly aslant to the direction of motion.

[11] $= \log_{sp}(m_2)$ characterizes the number of normal vectors being strongly aslant to the direction of motion.

[12] $= \log_{sp}(m_4 + m_3)$

[13] $= m_4 / |\mathcal{P}_g|$ characterizes the number of parallel normals relatively.

[14] $= (m_4 + m_3) / |\mathcal{P}_g|$

[15] $= \sum_h \min\{1, a_{g,h}\}$ holds the number of associations with strength > 0.

[16] $= \log_{sp}(\sum_h a_{g,h})$ holds the summed association strenghts.

The rest of the feature vector is three times a 12-dimensional vector for each of the associated tracks h_2, h_P, and h_a. Exemplary for h_2:

[17] $\in \{0, 1\}$ is 1 if the last measurement of h_2 was successful and 0 otherwise.

[18] $= \log_{sp}(a_{g,h_2})$ characterizes the association strenght.

[19] $= a_{g,h_2}/\sum_h a_{g,h}$ characterizes the association strenght relative to the summed strength.

[20] $= a_{g,h_2}/\max_h a_{g,h}$ characterizes the association strenght relative to the maximal strength.

[21] $\in \mathbb{N}$ characterizes when the last successful measurement of h_2 was made.

[22] $\in \mathbb{N}$ holds the age of h_2, limited by some upper bound.

[23] $= \log_{sp}(|\mathcal{P}_{h_2}|)$ characterizes the size of the appearance point cloud of h_2.

[24] $= \log_{sp}(|\mathcal{P}_{h_2}|/|\mathcal{P}_g|)$ characterizes the relative size of the appearance point cloud.

[25] $= e_{g,h_2,P}$ holds the point-to-plane error for the tracklet with the movement applied from h_2.

[26] $= e_{g,h_2,2}$ holds the point-to-point error for the tracklet with the movement applied from h_2.

[27] $= \log_{sp}(e_{g,h_2,P}/e_{g,P})$ characterizes the relative point-to-plane error increase when applying the movement of h_2.

[28] $= \log_{sp}(e_{g,h_2,2}/e_{g,2})$ characterizes the relative point-to-point error increase when applying the movement of h_2.

A.4.2 Association

For the tracklet g with associated track h, the 32-dimensional feature vector $\boldsymbol{f}_{g,h}$ is composed of similar values than $\boldsymbol{f}_g$:

[1] $= \sum_h \min\{1, a_{g,h}\}$

[2] $= \log_{sp}(a_{g,h})$

[3] $= \log_{sp}(\sum_i a_{g,i})$

[4] $= a_{g,h}/\sum_i a_{g,i}$

[5] $= a_{g,h}/\max_i a_{g,i}$

[6] $= e_{g,P}$

[7] $= e_{g,h,P}$

[8] $= \log_{sp}(e_{g,h,P}/e_{g,P})$

[9] $= \log_{sp}(e_{g,h,P}/e_{g,h_P,P})$

[10] $= e_{g,2}$

[11] $= e_{g,h,2}$

[12] $= \log_{sp}(e_{g,h,2}/e_{g,2})$

[13] $= \log_{sp}(e_{g,h,2}/e_{g,h_2,2})$

[14] $\in \{0,1,2,3\}$ characterizes when the last successful measurement was made.

[15] $\in \mathbb{N}$ characterizes when the last successful measurement of h was made.

[16] $= \log_{sp}(|\mathcal{P}_g|)$

[17] $= \log_{sp}(|\mathcal{P}_h|)$

[18] $= \log_{sp}(|\mathcal{P}_g| / |\mathcal{P}_h|)$

[19] $\in \{0, 1\}$ is 0 if the associated track is the static track and 1 otherwise.

[20] $\in \{0, 1\}$ is 0 if the only associated track is the static track and 1 otherwise.

[21] $= \log_{sp}\left(\left\| {}^t\rho'_g - {}^t\rho''_{g,h} \right\|\right)$ characterizes the pose difference between the tracklets pose and the applied movement of the associated track.

[22] $= \log_{sp}(\mathrm{d}_M({}^t\rho'_g, {}^t\rho''_{g,h}))$ characterizes the pose difference between the tracklets pose and the applied movement of the associated track using the pose-covariance of ${}_{t-3}^{t}\Sigma'_g$.

[23] $= \log_{sp}(\mathrm{d}_M({}^t\rho'_g, {}^t\rho''_{g,h}))$ characterizes the pose difference between the tracklets pose and the applied movement of the associated track using the pose-covariance of the associated track ${}_{*}^{t}\Sigma'_h$.

[24] $= \log_{sp}(m_4)$

[25] $= \log_{sp}(m_3)$

[26] $= \log_{sp}(m_2)$

[27] $= \log_{sp}(m_4 + m_3)$

[28] $= (m_4 + m_3)/(m_2 + m_1)$

[29] $= (m_4 + m_3 + m_2)/(m_1)$

[30] $= m_4/|\mathcal{P}_g|$

[31] $= (m_4 + m_3)/|\mathcal{P}_g|$

[32] characterizes for the bin of the motion-histogram with the highest value the average move in meters within the last three frames in direction of the normal vector.

A.5 Segmentation Error Calculation

This section describes an algorithm to calculate the number of pixels e_p that must be deleted from a pixel-set $\mathcal{S}$, such that for two segmentations $\mathcal{A} = \{\mathcal{S}_a \subseteq \mathcal{S}\}$ and $\mathcal{B} = \{\mathcal{S}_b \subseteq \mathcal{S}\}$ the latter is a refinement of the former (see Section 5.1.3). To ease notation, let $A := |\mathcal{A}|$ and $B := |\mathcal{B}|$.

The first step is to build an association matrix M from the two segmentations:

$$
M = \begin{pmatrix}
m_{00} & m_{01} & \cdots & m_{0A} \\
m_{10} & m_{11} & \cdots & m_{1A} \\
\vdots & \vdots & \ddots & \vdots \\
m_{B0} & m_{B1} & \cdots & m_{BA}
\end{pmatrix}
$$

Starting with a zero-initialized matrix, for each pixel $i \in \mathcal{S}$ the segmentation indices $a \in [0, \ldots, A]$ and $b \in [0, \ldots, B]$ are determined and the corresponding entry m_{ab} is increased by one. Index 0 thereby indicates that the pixel is not contained in any segment, an index > 0 indicates the segment this pixel is contained in. Hence, after processing all pixels, the sum of row and column 0 is equivalent to the number of pixels not contained in $\mathcal{A}$ and $\mathcal{B}$ respectively. Note that M simply transposes if $\mathcal{A}$ and $\mathcal{B}$ are swapped.

For an identical segmentation ($\mathcal{A} = \mathcal{B}$) the off-diagonal elements are zero. The diagonal elements m_{jj} directly specify the segment sizes and hence $\mathrm{tr}\{M\} = |\mathcal{S}|$ and $\mathrm{tr}\{M\} - m_{00} = A = B$. If $\mathcal{B}$ is a refinement of $\mathcal{A}$ (segments split into subparts) additional rows are added to M and the previous diagonal elements m_{jj} distribute within their column. Only if a segment $\mathcal{S}_b$ contains pixels of several $\mathcal{S}_a$ values distribute within rows. This is what the error e_p penalizes:

$$
e_p = \sum_{b=1}^{B} \left(\sum_{a=1}^{A} m_{ba} - \max\{m_{b1}, \ldots, m_{bA}\} \right) \tag{A.26}
$$

In case for each row b only one entry is non-zero, the inner sum equals the maximum and the error is zero. Not taken into account are row and column 0, i. e. pixels that are not contained in $\mathcal{A}$ or $\mathcal{B}$.

Bibliography

[Agr06]   M. Agrawal and K. Konolige: „Real-time Localization in Outdoor Environments using Stereo Vision and Inexpensive GPS". In Proceedings of *International Conference on Pattern Recognition*, pp. 1063–1068, 2006.

[Agu07]   C. Aguiar, S. Druon and A. Crosnier: „3D datasets segmentation based on local attribute variation". In Proceedings of *IEEE International Conference on Intelligent Robots and Systems*, pp. 3205–3210, 2007.

[Ary94]   S. Arya, D. M. Mount, N. S. Netanyahu, R. Silverman and A. Wu: „An optimal algorithm for approximate nearest neighbor searching". In Proceedings of *Fifth annual ACM-SIAM symposium on Discrete algorithms*, pp. 573–582, 1994.

[Ash98]   A. P. Ashbrook, R. B. Fisher, C. Robertson and N. Werghi: „Finding surface correspondence for object recognition and registration using pairwise geometric histograms". In Proceedings of *European Conference on Computer Vision*, vol. 2, pp. 674–686, 1998.

[Bab11]   B. Babenko, M.-H. Yang and S. Belongie: „Robust Object Tracking with Online Multiple Instance Learning". *IEEE Transactions on Pattern Analysis and Machine Intelligence*, vol. 33, pp. 1619–1632, 2011.

[Bac10]   A. Bachmann: *Dichte Objektsegmentierung in Stereobildfolgen.* Dissertation, Universität Karlsruhe (TH), Universitätsverlag, Karlsruhe, 2010. Schriftenreihe Institut für Mess- und Regelungstechnik, Nr. 015.

[Bad04]   H. Badino: „A Robust Approach for Ego-Motion Estimation Using a Mobile Stereo Platform". In Proceedings of *First International Workshop on Complex Motion*, pp. 198–208, 2004.

[Bad11]   H. Badino, D. Huber, Y. Park and T. Kanade: „Fast and Accurate Computation of Surface Normals from Range Images". In Proceedings of *IEEE International Conference on Robotics and Automation*, pp. 3084–3091, 2011.

[Bel99]   O. Bellon, A. Direne and L. Silva: „Edge detection to guide range image segmentation by clustering techniques". In Proceedings of *International Conference on Image Processing*, vol. 2, pp. 725–729, 1999.

[Bes88]   P. Besl and R. Jain: „Segmentation through variable-order surface fitting". *IEEE Transactions on Pattern Analysis and Machine Intelligence*, vol. 10 (2), pp. 167–192, 1988.

[Bes92]   P. Besl and H. McKay: „A method for registration of 3-D shapes". *IEEE Transactions on Pattern Analysis and Machine Intelligence*, vol. 14 (2), pp. 239–256, 1992.

[Böh08]   F. Böhringer: *Gleisselektive Ortung von Schienenfahrzeugen mit bordautonomer Sensorik*. Dissertation, Universität Karlsruhe (TH), Universitätsverlag, Karlsruhe, 2008. Schriftenreihe Institut für Mess- und Regelungstechnik, Nr. 011.

[Bos09]   M. Bosse and R. Zlot: „Continuous 3D Scan-Matching with a Spinning 2D Laser". In Proceedings of *IEEE International Conference on Robotics and Automation*, pp. 4312–4319, 2009.

[Bre10]   S. Brechtel, T. Gindele and R. Dillmann: „Recursive importance sampling for efficient grid-based occupancy filtering in dynamic environments". In Proceedings of *IEEE International Conference on Robotics and Automation*, pp. 3932–3938, 2010.

[BS87]   Y. Bar-Shalom: *Tracking and data association*. Academic Press Professional, Inc., San Diego, CA, USA, 1987.

[BS02]   Y. Bar-Shalom, T. Kirubarajan and X.-R. Li: *Estimation with Applications to Tracking and Navigation*. John Wiley & Sons, Inc., New York, NY, USA, 2002.

[Cam05]   J. Campbell, R. Sukthankar, I. Nourbakhsh and A. Pahwa: „A Robust Visual Odometry and Precipice Detection System Using Consumer-grade Monocular Vision". In Proceedings of *IEEE International Conference on Robotics and Automation*, pp. 3421–3427, 2005.

[Car05]   J. Cardoso and L. Corte-Real: „Toward a generic evaluation of image segmentation". *IEEE Transactions on Image Processing*, vol. 14 (11), pp. 1773–1782, 2005.

[Cen07a]   A. Censi: „An accurate closed-form estimate of ICP's covariance".
            In Proceedings of *IEEE International Conference on Robotics and
            Automation*, pp. 3167–3172, 2007.

[Cen07b]   A. Censi: „On achievable accuracy for range-finder localization".
            In Proceedings of *IEEE International Conference on Robotics and
            Automation*, pp. 4170–4175, 2007.

[Che91]   Y. Chen and G. Medioni: „Object modeling by registration of mul-
            tiple range images". In Proceedings of *IEEE International Confer-
            ence on Robotics and Automation*, vol. 3, pp. 2724–2729, 1991.

[Che06]   D. Chekhlov, M. Pupilli, W. Mayol-Cuevas and A. Calway:
            „Real-Time and Robust Monocular SLAM Using Predictive Multi-
            resolution Descriptors". In Proceedings of *International Symposium
            on Visual Computing*, pp. 276–285, 2006.

[Che07]   H. Chen and B. Bhanu: „3D free-form object recognition in range
            images using local surface patches". *Pattern Recognition Letters*,
            vol. 28 (10), pp. 1252–1262, 2007.

[Cou09]   J. Cousty, G. Bertrand, L. Najman and M. Couprie: „Watershed
            Cuts: Minimum Spanning Forests and the Drop of Water Principle".
            IEEE Transactions on Pattern Analysis and Machine Intelligence,
            vol. 31, pp. 1362–1374, 2009.

[Cox93]   I. J. Cox: „A review of statistical data association for motion corre-
            spondence". *International Journal of Computer Vision*, vol. 10 (1),
            pp. 53–66, 1993.

[Dal05]   N. Dalal and B. Triggs: „Histograms of Oriented Gradients for Hu-
            man Detection". In Proceedings of *IEEE International Conference
            on Computer Vision and Pattern Recognition (CVPR)*, vol. 2, pp.
            886–893, 2005.

[Dav08]   S. J. Davey, M. G. Rutten and B. Cheung: „A comparison of
            detection performance for several track-before-detect algorithms".
            EURASIP Journal on Advances in Signal Processing, vol. 2008, p.
            428036, 2008.

[Dic84]   E. D. Dickmanns, A. Zapp and K. D. Otto: „Ein Simulationskreis
            zur Entwicklung einer automatischen Fahrzeugführung mit bild-
            haften und inertialen Signalen". In Proceedings of *2. Symposium
            Simulationstechnik*, pp. 554–558, 1984.

[Dic88]   E. D. Dickmanns and A. Zapp: „Autonomous High Speed Road Vehicle Guidance by Computer Vision". In Proceedings of *10th International Federation of Automatic Control World Congress*, pp. 221–226, 1988.

[Dic92]   E. D. Dickmanns and B. D. Mysliwetz: „Recursive 3-D Road and Relative Ego-State Recognition". *IEEE Transactions on Pattern Analysis and Machine Intelligence*, vol. 14 (2), pp. 199–213, 1992.

[Dor06]   C. Dornhege and A. Kleiner: „Visual Odometry for Tracked Vehicles". In Proceedings of *IEEE International Workshop on Safety, Security and Rescue Robotics*, 2006.

[Dor07]   P. Dorninger and C. Nothegger: „3D Segmentation of Unstructured Point Clouds for Building Modelling". In Proceedings of *Photogrammetric Image Analysis*, vol. 35, pp. 191–196, 2007.

[Dou11]   B. Douillard, J. Underwood, N. Kuntz, V. Vlaskine, A. Quadros, P. Morton and A. Frenkel: „On the Segmentation of 3D LIDAR Point Clouds". In Proceedings of *IEEE International Conference on Robotics and Automation*, pp. 2798–2805, 2011.

[Dou12]   B. Douillard, A. Quadros, P. Morton, J. Underwood, M. DeDeuge, S. Hugosson, M. Hallstrom and T. Bailey: „Scan segments matching for pairwise 3D alignment". In Proceedings of *IEEE International Conference on Robotics and Automation*, pp. 3033–3040, 2012.

[Dud01]   R. O. Duda, P. E. Hart and D. G. Stork: *Pattern classification*. Wiley, 2nd. ed., 2001.

[Ess10]   A. Ess, K. Schindler, B. Leibe and L. Van Gool: „Object Detection and Tracking for Autonomous Navigation in Dynamic Environments". *The International Journal of Robotics Research*, vol. 29 (14), pp. 1707–1725, 2010.

[Far06]   B. Fardi, J. Dousa, G. Wanielik, B. Elias and A. Barke: „Obstacle Detection and Pedestrian Recognition Using A 3D PMD Camera". In Proceedings of *IEEE Intelligent Vehicles Symposium*, pp. 225–230, 2006.

[Fer10]   V. Ferrari, F. Jurie and C. Schmid: „From Images to Shape Models for Object Detection". *International Journal of Computer Vision*, vol. 87 (3), pp. 284–303, 2010.

[Fil02]   S. Filin: „Surface Clustering from Airborne Laser Scanning Data“. In Proceedings of *International Society for Photogrammetry and Remote Sensing Commission III Symposium*, pp. 119–124, 2002.

[Fly89]   P. Flynn and A. Jain: „On reliable curvature estimation“. In Proceedings of *IEEE International Conference on Computer Vision and Pattern Recognition (CVPR)*, pp. 110–116, 1989.

[Fox03]   V. Fox, J. Hightower, L. Liao, D. Schulz and G. Borriello: „Bayesian filtering for location estimation“. *IEEE Pervasive Computing*, vol. 2 (3), pp. 24–33, 2003.

[Fra09]   M. Frank, M. Plaue, H. Rapp, U. Köthe, B. Jähne and F. A. Hamprecht: „Theoretical and Experimental Error Analysis of Continuous-Wave Time-Of-Flight Range Cameras“. *Optical Engineering*, vol. 48 (1), pp. 013602–16, 2009.

[Gat08]   G. Gate and F. Nashashibi: „Using targets appearance to improve pedestrian classification with a laser scanner“. In Proceedings of *IEEE Intelligent Vehicles Symposium*, pp. 571–576, 2008.

[Gel03]   N. Gelfand, L. Ikemoto, S. Rusinkiewicz and M. Levoy: „Geometrically stable sampling for the ICP algorithm“. In Proceedings of *International Conference on 3-D Digital Imaging and Modeling*, pp. 260–267, 2003.

[Gon92]   R. C. Gonzalez and R. E. Woods: *Digital image processing*. World Student series. Addison-Wesley, Boston, MA, USA, 2nd. ed., 1992.

[Gri07]   G. Grisetti, C. Stachniss and W. Burgard: „Improved Techniques for Grid Mapping With Rao-Blackwellized Particle Filters“. *IEEE Transactions on Robotics*, vol. 23 (1), pp. 34–46, 2007.

[Gug63]   H. W. Guggenheimer: *Differential geometry*. MacGraw-Hill Series in Higher Mathematics. MacGraw-Hill, New York, USA, 1963.

[Guo11]   C. Guo, S. Mita, D. McAllester, W. Sato and L. Han: „Graph-Based 2D Road Representation of 3D Point Clouds for Intelligent Vehicles“. In Proceedings of *IEEE Intelligent Vehicles Symposium*, pp. 715–721, 2011.

[Han88]   J. Han and R. Volz: „Region grouping from a range image“. In Proceedings of *IEEE International Conference on Computer Vision and Pattern Recognition (CVPR)*, pp. 241–248, 1988.

[Har08]   A. Harrison and P. Newman: „High quality 3D laser ranging under general vehicle motion". In Proceedings of *IEEE International Conference on Robotics and Automation*, pp. 7–12, 2008.

[Him10]   M. Himmelsbach, F. von Hundelshausen and H. J. Wuensche: „Fast Segmentation of 3D Point Clouds for Ground Vehicles". In Proceedings of *IEEE Intelligent Vehicles Symposium*, pp. 560–565, 2010.

[Hof87]   R. Hoffman and A. K. Jain: „Segmentation and Classification of Range Images". *IEEE Transactions on Pattern Analysis and Machine Intelligence*, vol. PAMI-9 (5), pp. 608–620, 1987.

[Hol10]   D. Holz and S. Behnke: „Sancta Simplicitas – On the efficiency and achievable results of SLAM using ICP-Based Incremental Registration". In Proceedings of *IEEE International Conference on Robotics and Automation*, pp. 1380–1387, 2010.

[Hoo96]   A. Hoover, G. Jean-Baptiste, X. Jiang, P. J. Flynn, H. Bunke, D. B. Goldgof, K. Bowyer, D. W. Eggert, A. Fitzgibbon and R. B. Fisher: „An Experimental Comparison of Range Image Segmentation Algorithms". *IEEE Transactions on Pattern Analysis and Machine Intelligence*, vol. 18, pp. 673–689, 1996.

[Hor87]   B. K. P. Horn: „Closed-form solution of absolute orientation using unit quaternions". *Journal of the Optical Society of America*, vol. 4 (4), pp. 629–642, 1987.

[Jag07]   A. Jagannathan and E. Miller: „Three-Dimensional Surface Mesh Segmentation Using Curvedness-Based Region Growing Approach". *IEEE Transactions on Pattern Analysis and Machine Intelligence*, vol. 29 (12), pp. 2195–2204, 2007.

[Jep03]   A. D. Jepson, D. J. Fleet and T. F. El-Maraghi: „Robust Online Appearance Models for Visual Tracking". *IEEE Transactions on Pattern Analysis and Machine Intelligence*, vol. 25 (10), pp. 1296–1311, 2003.

[Joh99]   A. Johnson and M. Hebert: „Using spin images for efficient object recognition in cluttered 3D scenes". *IEEE Transactions on Pattern Analysis and Machine Intelligence*, vol. 21 (5), pp. 433–449, 1999.

[Jur05]   F. Jurie and B. Triggs: „Creating efficient codebooks for visual recognition". In Proceedings of *IEEE International Conference on Computer Vision*, vol. 1, pp. 604–610, 2005.

[Kab08]   G. Kable: *VW's new self-parking system*, Autocar, April 2008. http://www.autocar.co.uk/www.autocar.co.uk/News/NewsArticle/ AllCars/232417/.

[Kam08]   S. Kammel, J. Ziegler, B. Pitzer, M. Werling, T. Gindele, D. Jagzent, J. Schröder, M. Thuy, M. Goebl, F. von Hundelshausen, O. Pink, C. Frese and C. Stiller: „Team AnnieWAY's autonomous system for the 2007 DARPA Urban Challenge". *Journal of Field Robotics*, vol. 25 (9), pp. 615–639, 2008.

[Kap07]   A. Kapp: *Ein Beitrag zur Verbesserung und Erweiterung der Lidar-Signalverarbeitung für Fahrzeuge*. Dissertation, Universität Karlsruhe (TH), Universitätsverlag, Karlsruhe, 2007. Schriftenreihe Institut für Mess- und Regelungstechnik, Nr. 009.

[Kei02]   M. Keijzer, J. J. Merelo, G. Romero and M. Schoenauer: „Evolving Objects: A General Purpose Evolutionary Computation Library". *Artificial Evolution*, vol. 2310, pp. 829–888, 2002.

[Kid11]   K. Kidono, T. Miyasaka, A. Watanabe, T. Naito and J. Miura: „Pedestrian Recognition Using High-Definition LIDAR". In Proceedings of *IEEE Intelligent Vehicles Symposium*, pp. 405–410, 2011.

[Kit10]   B. Kitt, F. Moosmann and C. Stiller: „Moving on to Dynamic Environments: Visual Odometry using Feature Classification". In Proceedings of *IEEE International Conference on Intelligent Robots and Systems*, pp. 5551–5556, 2010.

[Kla08]   K. Klasing, D. Wollherr and M. Buss: „A clustering method for efficient segmentation of 3D laser data". In Proceedings of *IEEE International Conference on Robotics and Automation*, pp. 4043–4048, 2008.

[Kla09a]   K. Klasing, D. Althoff, D. Wollherr and M. Buss: „Comparison of surface normal estimation methods for range sensing applications". In Proceedings of *IEEE International Conference on Robotics and Automation*, pp. 3206–3211, 2009.

[Kla09b]   K. Klasing, D. Wollherr and M. Buss: „Realtime segmentation of range data using continuous nearest neighbors". In Proceedings of *IEEE International Conference on Robotics and Automation*, pp. 2431–2436, 2009.

[Kov99]   P. Kovesi: „Phase Preserving Denoising of Images". In Proceedings of *International Conference on Digital Image Computing: Techniques and Applications*, pp. 212–217, 1999.

[Lat10]   H. Lategahn, W. Derendarz, T. Graf, B. Kitt and J. Effertz: „Occupancy Grid Computation from Dense Stereo and Sparse Structure and Motion Points for Automotive Applications". In Proceedings of *IEEE Intelligent Vehicles Symposium*, pp. 819–824, 2010.

[Leo99]   J. J. Leonard, H. Jacob and S. Feder: „A computationally efficient method for large-scale concurrent mapping and localization". In Proceedings of *International Symposium on Robotics Research*, pp. 169–176, 1999.

[Lev10]   J. Levinson and S. Thrun: „Robust vehicle localization in urban environments using probabilistic maps". In Proceedings of *IEEE International Conference on Robotics and Automation*, pp. 4372–4378, 2010.

[Li07]   H. Li and R. Hartley: „The 3D-3D Registration Problem Revisited". In Proceedings of *IEEE International Conference on Computer Vision*, pp. 1–8, 2007.

[Lo09]   T.-W. R. Lo and J. P. Siebert: „Local feature extraction and matching on range images: 2.5D SIFT". *Computer Vision and Image Understanding*, vol. 113 (12), pp. 1235–1250, 2009. Special issue on 3D Representation for Object and Scene Recognition.

[Low04]   D. G. Lowe: „Distinctive image features from scale-invariant keypoints". *International Journal of Computer Vision*, vol. 60, pp. 91–110, 2004.

[Luc81]   B. D. Lucas and T. Kanade: „An Iterative Image Registration Technique with an Application to Stereo Vision (IJCAI)". In Proceedings of *International Joint Conference on Artificial Intelligence (IJCAI '81)*, pp. 674–679, 1981.

[Mak10]   A. Makadia and K. Daniilidis: „Spherical Correlation of Visual Representations for 3D Model Retrieval". *International Journal of Computer Vision*, vol. 89 (2-3), pp. 193–210, 2010.

[Mar01]   G. Marsden, M. McDonald and M. Brackstone: „Towards an understanding of adaptive cruise control". *Transportation Research Part C*, vol. 9 (1), pp. 33–51, 2001.

[Mat03]   I. Matthews, T. Ishikawa and S. Baker: „The Template Update Problem". In Proceedings of *British Machine Vision Conference*, pp. 810–815, 2003.

[May09]   S. May, S. Fuchs, D. Droeschel, D. Holz and A. Nüchter: „Robust 3D-Mapping with Time-of-Flight Cameras". In Proceedings of *IEEE International Conference on Intelligent Robots and Systems*, pp. 1673–1678, 2009.

[Mei98]   E. B. Meier and F. Ade: „Object Detection and Tracking in Range Image Sequences by Separation of Image Features". In Proceedings of *IEEE International Conference on Intelligent Vehicles*, pp. 176–181, 1998.

[Mia06]   A. Mian, M. Bennamoun and R. Owens: „Three-Dimensional Model-Based Object Recognition and Segmentation in Cluttered Scenes". *IEEE Transactions on Pattern Analysis and Machine Intelligence*, vol. 28 (10), pp. 1584–1601, 2006.

[Mic08]   O. Michailovich and A. Tannenbaum: „Segmentation of Tracking Sequences Using Dynamically Updated Adaptive Learning". *IEEE Transactions on Image Processing*, vol. 17 (12), pp. 2403–2412, 2008.

[Mon08]   M. Montemerlo, J. Becker, S. Bhat, H. Dahlkamp, D. Dolgov, S. Ettinger, D. Haehnel, T. Hilden, G. Hoffmann, B. Huhnke, D. Johnston, S. Klumpp, D. Langer, A. Levandowski, J. Levinson, J. Marcil, D. Orenstein, J. Paefgen, I. Penny, A. Petrovskaya, M. Pflueger, G. Stanek, D. Stavens, A. Vogt and S. Thrun: „Junior: The Stanford entry in the Urban Challenge". *Journal of Field Robotics*, vol. 25 (9), pp. 569–597, 2008.

[Moo06a]   F. Moosmann, D. Larlus and F. Jurie: „Learning Saliency Maps for Object Categorization". In Proceedings of *ECCV International Workshop on The Representation and Use of Prior Knowledge in Vision*, 2006.

[Moo06b]   F. Moosmann, B. Triggs and F. Jurie: „Fast Discriminative Visual Codebooks using Randomized Clustering Forests". In Proceedings of *NIPS - Neural Information Processing Systems*, pp. 985–992, 2006.

[Moo08]   F. Moosmann, E. Nowak and F. Jurie: „Randomized Clustering Forests for Image Classification". *IEEE Transactions on Pattern Analysis & Machine Intelligence*, vol. 30 (9), pp. 1632–1646, 2008.

[Moo09]   F. Moosmann, O. Pink and C. Stiller: „Segmentation of 3D Lidar Data in non-flat Urban Environments using a Local Convexity Criterion". In Proceedings of *IEEE Intelligent Vehicles Symposium*, pp. 215–220, 2009.

[Moo10]   F. Moosmann and T. Fraichard: „Motion Estimation from Range Images in Dynamic Outdoor Scenes". In Proceedings of *IEEE International Conference on Robotics and Automation*, pp. 142–147, 2010.

[Moo11a]   F. Moosmann and M. Sauerland: „Unsupervised Discovery of Object Classes in 3D Outdoor Scenarios". In Proceedings of *IEEE International Conference on Computer Vision Workshops*, pp. 1038–1044, 2011.

[Moo11b]   F. Moosmann and C. Stiller: „Velodyne SLAM". In Proceedings of *IEEE Intelligent Vehicles Symposium*, pp. 393–398, 2011.

[Nas08]   F. Nashashibi and A. Bargeton: „Laser-based vehicles tracking and classification using occlusion reasoning and confidence estimation". In Proceedings of *IEEE Intelligent Vehicles Symposium*, pp. 847–852, 2008.

[Nov08]   J. Novatnack and K. Nishino: „Scale-Dependent/Invariant Local 3D Shape Descriptors for Fully Automatic Registration of Multiple Sets of Range Images". In Proceedings of *European Conference on Computer Vision*, pp. 440–453, 2008.

[Nü07]   A. Nüchter, K. Lingemann, J. Hertzberg and H. Surmann: „6D SLAM—3D mapping outdoor environments: Research Articles". *Journal of Field Robotics*, vol. 24 (8–9), pp. 699–722, 2007.

[Pet09]   A. Petrovskaya and S. Thrun: „Model based vehicle detection and tracking for autonomous urban driving". *Autonomous Robots*, vol. 26 (2-3), pp. 123–139, 2009.

[Pfe10]   D. Pfeiffer and U. Franke: „Efficient representation of traffic scenes by means of dynamic stixels". In Proceedings of *IEEE Intelligent Vehicles Symposium*, pp. 217–224, 2010.

[Pin09]   O. Pink, F. Moosmann and A. Bachmann: „Visual Features for Vehicle Localization and Ego-Motion Estimation". In Proceedings of *IEEE Intelligent Vehicles Symposium*, pp. 254–260, 2009.

[Pre85]   F. P. Preparata and M. I. Shamos: *Computational geometry: an introduction*. Texts and monographs in computer science. Springer-Verlag, New York, NY, USA, 1st. ed., 1985.

[Qiu09]   D. Qiu, S. May and A. Nüchter: *GPU-Accelerated Nearest Neighbor Search for 3D Registration*. In *Computer Vision Systems*, vol. 5815 of *Lecture Notes in Computer Science*, pp. 194–203. Springer-Verlag, Berlin, Heidelberg, Germany, 2009.

[Rab06]   T. Rabbani, F. van den Heuvel and G. Vosselmann: „Segmentation of point clouds using smoothness constraint". In Proceedings of *International Archives of the Photogrammetry, Remote Sensing and Spatial Information Sciences*, vol. 36, pp. 248–253, 2006.

[Reu09]   S. Reuter and K. Dietmayer: „Fuzzy estimation and segmentation for laser range scans". In Proceedings of *International Conference on Information Fusion*, pp. 1974–1981, 2009.

[Rus01]   S. Rusinkiewicz and M. Levoy: „Efficient variants of the ICP algorithm". In Proceedings of *International Conference on 3-D Digital Imaging and Modeling*, pp. 145–152, 2001.

[Rus09]   R. B. Rusu, N. Blodow and M. Beetz: „Fast Point Feature Histograms (FPFH) for 3D Registration". In Proceedings of *IEEE International Conference on Robotics and Automation*, pp. 3212–3217, 2009.

[Sab96]   B. Sabata and J. K. Aggarwal: „Surface Correspondence and Motion Computation from a Pair of Range Images". *Computer Vision and Image Understanding*, vol. 63 (2), pp. 232–250, 1996.

[Sal07]   J. Salvi, C. Matabosch, D. Fofi and J. Forest: „A review of recent range image registration methods with accuracy evaluation". *Image and Vision Computing*, vol. 25 (5), pp. 578–596, 2007.

[Sch08]   T. Schamm, J. M. Zöllner, S. Vacek, J. Schröder and R. Dillmann: „Obstacle detection with a Photonic Mixing Device-camera in autonomous vehicles". *International Journal of Intelligent Systems Technologies and Applications*, vol. 5 (3/4), pp. 315–324, 2008.

[Sch10]   B. Schwarz: „Lidar: Mapping the world in 3D". *Nature Photonics*, vol. 4 (7), pp. 429–430, 2010.

[Seg09]   A. Segal, D. Hähnel and S. Thrun: „Generalized-ICP". In Proceedings of *Robotics: Science and Systems*, 2009.

[Sha49]   C. E. Shannon: „Communication in the Presence of Noise". *Proceedings of the Institute of Radio Engineers*, vol. 37 (1), pp. 10–21, 1949.

[Sha01]   L. G. Shapiro and G. C. Stockman: *Computer vision*. Prentice Hall, Upper Saddle River, NJ, 2001.

[Sha09]   L. Shapira, S. Shalom, A. Shamir, D. Cohen-Or and H. Zhang: „Contextual Part Analogies in 3D Objects". *International Journal of Computer Vision*, vol. 89 (2–3), pp. 309–326, 2009.

[Sid00]   H. Sidenbladh, M. J. Black and D. J. Fleet: „Stochastic Tracking of 3D Human Figures Using 2D Image Motion". In Proceedings of *European Conference on Computer Vision*, pp. 702–718, 2000.

[Spi10]   L. Spinello, R. Triebel and R. Siegwart: „Multiclass Multimodal Detection and Tracking in Urban Environments". *The International Journal of Robotics Research*, vol. 29 (12), pp. 1498–1515, 2010.

[Ste08]   D. Steinhauser, O. Ruepp and D. Burschka: „Motion segmentation and scene classification from 3D LIDAR data". In Proceedings of *IEEE Intelligent Vehicles Symposium*, pp. 398–403, 2008.

[Ste10]   B. Steder, G. Grisetti and W. Burgard: „Robust place recognition for 3D range data based on point features". In Proceedings of *IEEE International Conference on Robotics and Automation*, pp. 1400–1405, 2010.

[Ste11]   B. Steder, R. B. Rusu, K. Konolige and W. Burgard: „Point Feature Extraction on 3D Range Scans Taking into Account Object Boundaries". In Proceedings of *IEEE International Conference on Robotics and Automation*, pp. 2601–2608, 2011.

[Sti06]   C. Stiller: *Grundlagen der Mess- und Regelungstechnik*. Shaker-Verlag, Aachen, Germany, oct 2006.

[Str04]   D. Streller and K. Dietmayer: „Multiple hypothesis classification with laser range finders". In Proceedings of *IEEE International Conference on Intelligent Transportation Systems*, pp. 195–200, 2004.

[Thr03]   S. Thrun: „Learning Occupancy Grid Maps with Forward Sensor
           Models". *Autonomous Robots*, vol. 15 (2), pp. 111–127, 2003.

[Thr04]   S. Thrun, Y. Liu, D. Koller, A. Y. Ng, Z. Ghahramani and
           H. Durrant-Whyte: „Simultaneous Localization and Mapping with
           Sparse Extended Information Filters". *The International Journal of
           Robotics Research*, vol. 23 (7-8), pp. 693–716, 2004.

[Thr05]   S. Thrun, W. Burgard and D. Fox: *Probabilistic robotics*. Intelligent
           robotics and autonomous agents. MIT Press, September 2005.

[Tom98]   C. Tomasi and R. Manduchi: „Bilateral filtering for gray and color
           images". In Proceedings of *IEEE International Conference on Com-
           puter Vision*, pp. 839–846, 1998.

[Uij10]   J. Uijlings, A. Smeulders and R. Scha: „Real-Time Visual Concept
           Classification". *IEEE Transactions on Multimedia*, vol. 12 (7), pp.
           665–681, 2010.

[Urm08]   C. Urmson, J. Anhalt, H. Bae, J. A. D. Bagnell, C. Baker, R. E. Bit-
           tner, T. Brown, M. N. Clark, M. Darms, D. Demitrish, J. Dolan,
           D. Duggins, D. Ferguson, T. Galatali, C. M. Geyer, M. Gittle-
           man, S. Harbaugh, M. Hebert, T. Howard, S. Kolski, M. Likhachev,
           B. Litkouhi, A. Kelly, M. McNaughton, N. Miller, J. Nickolaou,
           K. Peterson, B. Pilnick, R. Rajkumar, P. Rybski, V. Sadekar,
           B. Salesky, Y.-W. Seo, S. Singh, J. M. Snider, J. C. Struble, A. T.
           Stentz, M. Taylor, W. R. L. Whittaker, Z. Wolkowicki, W. Zhang
           and J. Ziglar: „Autonomous driving in urban environments: Boss
           and the Urban Challenge". *Journal of Field Robotics*, vol. 25 (8),
           pp. 425–466, 2008.

[vdV10]   J. van de Ven, F. Ramos and G. Tipaldi: „An integrated probabilis-
           tic model for scan-matching, moving object detection and motion
           estimation". In Proceedings of *IEEE International Conference on
           Robotics and Automation*, pp. 887–894, 2010.

[Vu08]   T.-D. Vu, J. Burlet and O. Aycard: „Grid-based localization and on-
           line mapping with moving objects detection and tracking: new re-
           sults". In Proceedings of *IEEE Intelligent Vehicles Symposium*, pp.
           684–689, 2008.

[Wah03]   E. Wahl, G. Hillenbrand and G. Hirzinger: „Surflet-pair-relation his-
           tograms: a statistical 3D-shape representation for rapid classifica-

tion". In Proceedings of *International Conference on 3-D Digital Imaging and Modeling*, pp. 474–481, 2003.

[Wan04]   C.-C. Wang: *Simultaneous Localization, Mapping and Moving Object Tracking*. PhD thesis, Robotics Institute, Carnegie Mellon University, Pittsburgh, PA, April 2004.

[Wen05]   S. Wender, M. Schoenherr, N. Kaempchen and K. Dietmayer: „Classification of laserscanner measurements at intersection scenarios with automatic parameter optimization". In Proceedings of *IEEE Intelligent Vehicles Symposium*, pp. 94–99, 2005.

[Wen08]   S. Wender and K. Dietmayer: „3D vehicle detection using a laser scanner and a video camera". *Intelligent Transport Systems, IET*, vol. 2 (2), pp. 105–112, 2008.

[Whi01]   D. Whitley: „An Overview of Evolutionary Algorithms: Practical Issues and Common Pitfalls". *Information and Software Technology*, vol. 43, pp. 817–831, 2001.

[Wie64]   N. Wiener: *Extrapolation, Interpolation, and Smoothing of Stationary Time Series*. The MIT Press, March 1964.

[Zad65]   L. A. Zadeh: „Fuzzy Sets". *Information and Control*, vol. 8 (3), pp. 338–353, 1965.

[Zav09]   A. Zavodny, P. Flynn and X. Chen: „Region Extraction in Large-Scale Urban LIDAR Data". In Proceedings of *International Conference on Computer Vision Workshop on 3-D Digital Imaging and Modeling*, pp. 1801–1808, 2009.

[Zha96]   Y. J. Zhang: „A survey on evaluation methods for image segmentation". *Pattern Recognition*, vol. 29 (8), pp. 1335–1346, 1996.

Schriftenreihe
Institut für Mess- und Regelungstechnik
Karlsruher Institut für Technologie
(1613-4214)

Die Bände sind unter www.ksp.kit.edu als PDF frei verfügbar oder als Druckausgabe bestellbar.